READING, WRITING, and RIGOR

READING, WRITING, and RIGOR

Helping Students Achieve Greater Depth of Knowledge in Literacy

NANCY BOYLES

Alexandria, VA USA

1703 N. Beauregard St. • Alexandria, VA 22311-1714 USA
Phone: 800-933-2723 or 703-578-9600 • Fax: 703-575-5400
Website: www.ascd.org • E-mail: member@ascd.org
Author guidelines: www.ascd.org/write

Deborah S. Delisle, *Executive Director;* Stefani Roth, *Publisher;* Genny Ostertag, *Director, Content Acquisitions;* Carol Collins, *Acquisitions Editor;* Julie Houtz, *Director, Book Editing & Production;* Darcie Russell, *Senior Associate Editor;* Masie Chong, *Graphic Designer;* Mike Kalyan, *Director, Production Services;* Valerie Younkin, *Production Designer;* Kelly Marshall, *Senior Production Specialist*

All web links in this book are correct as of the publication date below but may have become inactive or otherwise modified since that time. If you notice a deactivated or changed link, please e-mail books@ascd.org with the words "Link Update" in the subject line. In your message, please specify the web link, the book title, and the page number on which the link appears.

PAPERBACK ISBN: 978-1-4166-2555-1   ASCD product #118026   n4/18

PDF E-BOOK ISBN: 978-1-4166-2556-8; see Books in Print for other formats.

Quantity discounts are available: e-mail programteam@ascd.org or call 800-933-2723, ext. 5773, or 703-575-5773. For desk copies, go to www.ascd.org/deskcopy.

Library of Congress Cataloging-in Publication Data
Names: Boyles, Nancy. N., 1948–author.
Title: Reading, writing, and rigor : helping students achieve greater depth of knowledge in
   literacy / Nancy Boyles.
Other titles: Helping students achieve greater depth of knowledge in literacy
Description: Alexandria, Virginia : ASCD, 2018. | Includes bibliographical references and index.
Identifiers: LCCN 2017057162 (print) | LCCN 2018013511 (ebook) | ISBN 9781416625568 (PDF) |
   ISBN 9781416625551 | ISBN 9781416625551 (pbk.)
Subjects: LCSH: Language arts—United States. | Language arts—Standards—United States. |
   Language arts—United States. | Reading—Ability testing. | Literacy—United States.
Classification: LCC LB1576 (ebook) | LCC LB1576 .B547 2018 (print) | DDC 379.2/40973—dc23
LC record available at https://lccn.loc.gov/2017057162

27 26 25 24 23 22 21 20 19 18   1 2 3 4 5 6 7 8 9 10 11 12

To Tessa

For the joy you bring to our family—

May your teachers always recognize your infinite gifts

as a learner and inspire you to dream big.

And may you love books as much as your Auntie.

Smile on!

READING, WRITING, and RIGOR

Introduction
Wanted: Rigor in Literacy

I had just completed a full-day workshop and was packing my books for the trip back to the airport when the only teacher who remained in the room hurried toward me. "Could you look at these questions?" she asked, waving a sheet of paper. "My principal is doing a walk-through tomorrow. He's looking for rigor. Do you think my questions are hard enough?"

I glanced at the clock, which announced a tight timeline if my flight departed on schedule. But I could at least take a quick glance. I found questions that really were pretty good, with lots of inferential thinking required. So, if her principal defined rigor as questions beyond the literal level, I expected this teacher would fare reasonably well. The problem is, however, that "hard questions" miss the essence of rigor.

Defining Rigor in Literacy

What exactly is *rigor*? Teachers and administrators toss the term about as if it were education's golden fleece: If we could just get more rigor in our classrooms, all would be well with the world. There are pleas for more rigorous curriculum, rigor in assessments, rigor in the content areas and the questions teachers ask. Once I even heard a teacher ask her students to "sit with rigor." (I'm still contemplating that one.) The term is often used together with words like *high expectations, challenge, complexity,* and *deep thinking.*

It's easier to find synonyms or words aligned with rigor than it is to find a good definition of it. In fact, a good definition of rigor is especially hard to come by as it relates to an academic area like literacy. Here's a general definition that I like, a place to start:

> Rigor is the result of work that challenges students' thinking in new and interesting ways. It occurs when they are encouraged toward a sophisticated understanding of fundamental ideas and are driven by curiosity to discover what they don't know. (Sztabnik, 2015)

The Rigor Is in the Answer

> We need to acknowledge that rigor doesn't reside in questions, but in answers. Questions and other tasks provide the *opportunity* for rigor; it's the answers that show the rigor.

The phrase "sophisticated understanding of fundamental ideas" draws attention as the essence of rigor because it matches other descriptors we often hear. But just focusing on synonyms would miss the most important word here: *result*. Rigor is the result, or *outcome*, of work students do. So right from the get-go, we need to acknowledge that rigor doesn't reside in questions, but in answers. Questions and other tasks provide the *opportunity* for rigor; it's the answers that *show* the rigor.

We should also pay closer attention to the word *toward*: students are encouraged "*toward* a sophisticated understanding." To me, this means that all rigor is not something that is already at the point of "sophisticated understanding," but that worthy learning opportunities intentionally move students in this direction. There are steps along the way.

Here is how I define rigor in literacy, accounting for four specific steps. Rigor in literacy is (1) precision in identifying the best textual evidence, (2) independence in applying literacy skills and concepts accurately, (3) insight into content and craft based on depth of reasoning, and (4) creativity in synthesizing information, often from multiple sources or points of view.

The Rigor of Each Depth of Knowledge

How did Depth of Knowledge (DOK) become part of our literacy landscape? It all began with Norman Webb (Webb, 2002). He developed DOK as a process for examining the alignment between standards and standardized assessments, using four key criteria, or steps. Those four criteria serve the same purpose today in analyzing items on new standards-based assessments. But we now apply these criteria to the analysis of curriculum, as well: How complex is the task? We recognize that different kinds of tasks require different depths of knowledge, from shallow to great.

The four steps in my definition match the four levels of Depth of Knowledge, as shown in Figure 1. Notice that each DOK and its associated form of rigor are linked to the ones that come before and after. Evidence, associated with DOK 1, is the foundation for everything that follows. Skills, DOK 2, require evidence for suitable elaboration. Insight, associated with DOK 3, is derived from the thoughtful application of skills. The creativity that results from synthesizing information, associated with DOK 4, grows out of the unique interpretation of insights.

Measuring the Depths of Knowledge on Standards-Based Assessments, Then and Now

The way new assessments measure Depth of Knowledge will be explored one level at a time in subsequent chapters. But for now, let's look in the rearview mirror to see how past assessments have evaluated students' literacy thinking.

FIGURE 1 | Defining the Rigor in Each Depth of Knowledge

DOK	Rigor
Level 1: Recalling and reproducing information	Precision in identifying the best textual evidence
Level 2: Applying skills or knowledge of concepts	Independence in applying literacy skills and concepts accurately
Level 3: Employing strategic thinking and reasoning	Insight into content and craft based on depth of reasoning
Level 4: Using extended thinking	Creativity in synthesizing information, often from multiple sources or points of view

In 2012, RAND published a working paper (Yuan & Le, 2012) that showed all too clearly why new assessments were needed. Not so long ago, state tests did little to evaluate deep thinking, even when the states' standards may have included that level of knowledge. In an examination of 17 state tests administered to students before the arrival of the Common Core, approximately 80 percent of all items for both reading and writing measured only Depths of Knowledge 1 and 2, with just 20 percent testing DOK 3 and DOK 4. This means that former state assessments most frequently measured students' ability to recall details and apply skills instead of asking them to analyze, critique, or extend their thinking. In fact, DOK 4 was hardly represented at all on reading items. This meant that students were rarely expected to read multiple sources and synthesize information in their responses.

But this situation is changing. A study published in the journal *Education Next* (Peterson, Barrows, & Gift, 2016) finds that since 2011, 45 states have changed their assessments and raised the levels at which students are considered "proficient." That action means more emphasis on rigor in students' responses, deeper levels of knowledge—and stress for teachers.

Where Our Thinking About DOK Has Gone Off Track

We see those higher levels of proficiency and want to prepare our students for the rigor they will need to demonstrate on these new, harder tests. But we don't know where to begin. And if we're completely honest, we don't even know what questions at each Depth of Knowledge will look like on these assessments.

For a few years after the arrival of the Common Core, we did not have good models of the kinds of questions students would probably encounter on standards-based assessments. Initially, a few representative items at each grade level appeared in Appendix B of the Common Core (http://www.corestandards

.org/assets/Appendix_B.pdf). But these became outdated as soon as test-builders such as the Smarter Balanced Assessment Consortium (SBAC) and the Partnership for Assessment of Readiness for College and Careers (PARCC) began designing the "real" assessments. Even the items on these measures weren't too reliable at first. Test length, question types, and scoring have all undergone numerous transformations.

Other missteps occurred as well. One early myth was "DOK 4 is project-based." This assumption led to asking students to complete performance tasks like "Draw a map of your dream bedroom" or "Create a life-size model of Sarah from *Sarah Plain and Tall*." We now know that such tasks were off base because they didn't draw on textual knowledge in substantial ways.

Performance-based tasks as they appear on new standards-based tests are a collection of complex comprehension questions and extended writing tasks that often require students to synthesize information from multiple texts and use that information to answer questions and then generate a product that is uniquely their own. Unfortunately, this misunderstanding about performance tasks has not been the only rabbit hole we've tumbled down. Some other guidelines have been too general in nature, and sometimes even misleading.

One example of information that was too general to be helpful for new assessments is Norman Webb's chart of DOK Question Stems (see http://svesd .net/files/DOK_Question_Stems.pdf). In the chart, the bullet points listed under each DOK are appropriate to the designated level of thinking but in some cases are not a good match for the kinds of tasks students will encounter on assessments. Several of the stems on this chart lack suitable specificity: "What is your interpretation of this text?" "Write a research paper on a topic." "What can you say about _____?" Students will be given more direct guidance than this on new assessments, and we should provide clearer direction for the tasks *we* assign as well.

Those wheels of verbs sorted into categories for each DOK level haven't been very helpful, either. Remember that Depth of Knowledge isn't about the *verb* but about what students *do* with that verb. For example, *describe* doesn't fit neatly into one category. Students might be asked to *describe* a character based on details retrieved directly from a text—a task that would represent a low level of knowledge. Or they could be asked to *describe* similarities and differences in the way an author portrays characters in two different texts—a much more robust task. Depth of Knowledge is about the *task*, not the *process*; it's about the literacy understanding students have acquired in relation to a specific text.

This attribute is what makes Depth of Knowledge different from Bloom's taxonomy. Bloom emphasizes the kind of thinking students do, the *process*. DOK focuses on the outcome of students' thinking, the *product*. Students will never "master" a Depth of Knowledge because the DOK 2 product they create based on their knowledge of an easy text may be very different from what they generate for DOK 2 when the text is more difficult.

Teaching Smart

Although reliable information on standards-based assessment items was once unavailable, that is no longer the case. Over the last couple of years, a side-by-side comparison of items from one assessment to another shows more similarities than differences. In other words, we can be relatively confident that the types of questions on last year's test will appear again this year.

Many sample assessment items are available. I rely on SBAC Resources and Documentation: http://www.smarterbalanced.org/assessments/practice -and-training-tests/resources-and-documentation/ and PARCC Released Items: https://parcc-assessment.org/practice-tests/. Smarter Balanced and PARCC were the first organizations to develop assessments based on the Common Core, and other publishers seem to have followed their lead in designing similar measures. To make it easier for you to examine question types, a list of sites with released items is provided on page 198 of Chapter 7, Teaching Tools and Resources.

To help you teach smart, this book will carefully examine sample items for each Depth of Knowledge—not so you can create other questions in their image and teach to the test, but so you can enhance your instruction and help students develop key literacy skills that will empower them as readers and writers. The goal is to teach to the rigor! A tool for teachers, Protocol for Analyzing Assessment Items, is provided on page 195 of Chapter 7 to make this item analysis systematic and as practical as possible. Notice that this analysis begins with understanding the item and ends with understanding the instruction.

Getting On Track for Depths of Knowledge

Teachers want to know, "What can we do in our classrooms to make Depth of Knowledge real for kids?" First, I suggest that we honor rigor at all the Depths of Knowledge. If we view rigor as applying only to DOK 3 and DOK 4, we will have overlooked foundational textual knowledge that students need to fully grasp the deeper complexities of a text.

We should hold our students accountable to rigor at *all* knowledge levels and ourselves to practices that promote rigor. In the past, we too often made the mistake of omitting tasks that tapped the rigor of DOK 3 and DOK 4—a serious oversight, for sure. But if we don't respect the rigor required for DOK 1 and DOK 2, students will be unprepared to grapple with the rigor of tasks that are more challenging.

We need to proceed with care in making these midcourse corrections. Many teachers perceive the rigor associated with Depth of Knowledge 1 as so basic that it barely warrants their time to invest in it. The rigor of Depth of Knowledge 2 relates to building skills and concepts, another area where teachers fall back on a long history of instructional experience. Doing so masks the urgency of more effective teaching of skills.

If we view rigor as applying only to DOK 3 and DOK 4, we will have overlooked foundational textual knowledge that students need to fully grasp the deeper complexities of a text.

We don't have to throw out everything we've ever known about teaching and learning to get rigor right. Rather, the charge is to rethink our current practices, tweaking as necessary and enriching our teaching with a few new high-yield strategies that have great turnaround potential.

Depth of Knowledge 3 is probably the weakest link in the pursuit of rigor because so many teachers are unclear about what rigor at this level entails—not to mention their even more limited understanding of how to support it. Then there's the rigor of Depth of Knowledge 4, which may be more familiar because of its connection to performance-based tasks that require the integration of information from multiple sources. Still, when teachers are left on their own to design similar performance tasks, it is apparent that their insights into what constitutes a good text-connection lesson and extended writing task may be off the mark.

The good news is that these issues are fixable—and we don't have to throw out everything we've ever known about teaching and learning to get rigor right. Rather, the charge is to rethink our current practices, tweaking as necessary and enriching our teaching with a few new high-yield strategies that have great turnaround potential. We can achieve this goal by viewing the rigor of each Depth of Knowledge through various lenses:

- Aligning rigor and standards
- Aligning rigor and text complexity
- Aligning rigor and close reading
- Aligning rigor and student interaction
- Aligning rigor and the reading-writing connection
- Aligning rigor and formative assessment

Aligning Rigor and Standards

Any discussion of rigor—or just about anything else in literacy education today—needs to begin with standards. We need a context for our new assessments and the learning opportunities we provide. In other words, what are we aiming for?

Despite some controversy over the Common Core, no one is challenging the need for literacy standards in one form or another. Most states have now adapted or modified the original CCSS document to reflect the needs of their population. But in truth, these new standards, regardless of what we title them, have helped both teachers and students reach higher in meeting literacy goals. We know this because the assessments designed to measure students' literacy knowledge based on these new-era standards do, indeed, raise the bar for what counts as top-of-the-line literacy performance.

The Expectations Set by the New Standards

What do these new standards ask of students? Some of the expectations are the same as earlier ones because many of the essentials of text analysis are just what they've always been: identifying details, story elements, main ideas, themes—the list goes on. This is the "what" of reading: *What* is the author saying? Teachers have been holding students accountable to standards such as these for as long as we all can remember, which leads some educators to conclude that these new standards are simply the same old cake with a different frosting. But that would be a naïve conclusion that overlooks much of the rigor expected of students from these new standards.

Beyond the expectation that students will understand the content of what they read, today's more demanding standards also ask students to attend to the crafting and structure of a text, as well as next steps in applying new knowledge: *How* is the author communicating meaning and the integration of knowledge and ideas? *Why* is the author providing this information? What can you *do* with this knowledge? These are areas often omitted by teachers. Even elementary students, and certainly middle school students, now need to examine these more nuanced dimensions of a text.

If your state doesn't code standards exactly as the Common Core codes them, know that elements of text analysis are generally consistent wherever you may live. For example, what CCSS calls "College and Career Readiness Standard 2: Determining central ideas" might be labeled as something else in your corner of the world, but it still taps the same kind of textual knowledge.

What's "Hard"?

One final thought about standards: teachers often complain to me that these new standards are "hard." To resolve this complaint, we need to be honest with ourselves: Are they hard because we've provided instruction around these standards and students still don't "get it"? Or are they hard because there are things we have not taught related to the new standards, or not taught in a way that taps deeper levels of thinking? It's this second possibility that we must face squarely if we aim to make a difference going forward.

Aligning Rigor and Text Complexity

Getting the right reading materials into students' hands is an essential first step in successful curriculum implementation, and that sometimes feels like half the battle when teaching a lesson. Aligning rigor and text complexity should always be a consideration when planning for literacy instruction. We can begin with the complexities defined for us in Appendix A of the Common Core (http://www .corestandards.org/assets/Appendix_A.pdf). There are both qualitative and quantitative complexities. The qualitative complexities include the following:

- Knowledge demands: The amount of prior knowledge a text requires
- Meaning: The understanding we want students to gain from a text
- Language: The vocabulary of a text
- Structure: The way a text is organized

If your state doesn't code standards exactly as the Common Core codes them, know that elements of text analysis are generally consistent wherever you may live.

But there are other qualitative complexities to consider, too. If we want to maximize the rigor at each Depth of Knowledge, we need to consider what makes a text ideal for each DOK. These additional complexities will be addressed in the following chapters.

Then there's the matter of quantitative complexity. A major shift that has come about in the pursuit of greater rigor through new standards is the expectation that students will read text that is not just more difficult to understand, with more sophisticated language and structure, but that also represents a higher readability level. Readability is a quantitative measure, such as Lexile, which is calculated by sentence length and word frequency (see the Lexile Analyzer at https://lexile.com/analyzer/). A text's Lexile number does not consider the qualitative complexities of the text nor does it consider how engaging the text might be for a group of students.

In a recent blog post, one notable literacy expert, Timothy Shanahan (2016), offers two suggestions for teaching with complex text:

- Make sure that kids are getting opportunities to read texts that are at the specified reading levels set by your standards. These texts are likely to be somewhat hard to read—in terms of decoding, vocabulary meaning, grasping what the author is explicitly saying. As such, they might not be the best texts for close reading.

- When you do ask kids to read texts that are hard to read, you need to be prepared to scaffold—to give students supports that will help them to make sense of the text; helping with decoding, preteaching vocabulary, breaking down sentences, connecting pronoun referents, making sense of organization, etc.

Although Shanahan's plea for "texts that are hard to read" contradicts current practices like guided reading that are founded on the precise leveling of students and placement into "just right" books, we should be open to his logic. If we don't offer students the opportunity to grapple with text that is more complex, we can hardly be surprised when they fall further and further behind. But let's be sensible about this: there will likely be a line in the sand for many readers, especially young students and those who struggle with fluency, at which point a text simply can't work. They will not be able to retrieve evidence demonstrating any Depth of Knowledge because they can barely recognize the words.

To make sure the text students read is challenging but not too frustrating, perhaps we need a new definition of "just right." We should offer students substantially complex texts for whole-class lessons where the teacher is actively part of the process and able to guide and scaffold. When students are reading in small groups, reasonable differentiation should be considered. But take a chance on text that might be a bit more challenging than one you would have considered in the past. Careful scaffolding and manageable challenge will push students to "level up."

Aligning Rigor and Close Reading

We should also consider the relationship between rigor and instruction. Given that close reading is so often cited as a key instructional approach to support students' achievement of standards and understanding of complex text, we'll need to examine close reading for its effect on the rigor of each Depth of Knowledge (see page 7, https://parcc-assessment.org/content/uploads/2017/11/PARCCMCFELALiteracyAugust2012_FINAL.pdf).

I am a passionate advocate of close reading. Through close reading we endeavor to build students' capacity for deep textual analysis. We want readers to probe both big ideas and subtle nuances of content and craft. But in the end, close reading is simply the *process*, the way students engage with a text *during* reading.

New assessments have now addressed what students should be able to do *after* reading, though the close reading path to getting there is less clear. In this book, we will examine differences in close reading practices at each Depth of Knowledge, but we can begin to solve this riddle by identifying principles of instruction before, during, and after close reading that prevail across all levels.

Before close reading. We know by examining the teacher's manual in many published programs that experts in the past have advocated heavy-duty scaffolding before reading: lots of personal connections, predictions about what the text will probably be about, building background knowledge, introducing vocabulary, and in the primary grades, a picture walk—all to enhance students' comprehension. For close reading, these practices may no longer be the best approach. We want students to get their information from the text, not the teacher, to develop independence rather than dependence.

During reading. In the recent past, the approach during reading has been for students to find the evidence for a specific comprehension skill that was a good match for the text. In fact, we teachers often chose a text based on its potential to advance a particular skill, and during reading we guided students to retrieve evidence related to this single focus. We used the text as a vehicle for teaching the aligned skill and then often moved on to a different text or passage to reinforce the same objective.

What does close reading say about using a text during reading in this way? For what Depths of Knowledge is identifying evidence for a specific focus a good idea? When should support during reading guide students to examine evidence more broadly? Different Depths of Knowledge call for different approaches to making meaning during close reading.

After reading. For many years, the time after reading has been characterized by asking questions—sometimes long lists of questions—that students answer in writing. But when teachers just ask questions and expect students to "publish" their thinking on paper, is this instruction or assessment? What might instructional scaffolding look like after close reading at different Depths of Knowledge?

In the chapters that follow, we will examine rigor before, during, and after reading for each Depth of Knowledge as it relates to student interaction, the reading-writing connection, and formative assessment.

Aligning Rigor and Student Interaction

We hear a lot about student engagement and hardly need to be convinced of its importance. But "engagement" is difficult to measure. That quiet kid in the corner *looks* like he's tuned in, but he hasn't said a word throughout the entire lesson. Is he just shy and reluctant to participate, or is his mind miles away, contemplating the soccer game scheduled for after school? Although it's hard to quantify engagement, we can more easily assess *interaction*: To what extent are students interacting with the text, their peers, and their teacher?

Interaction isn't always a synonym for *discussion*. Interaction can mean opportunities for student responses, from a simple "thumbs up" to extended discourse around a literacy-related problem—and many things in between. Where will these various kinds of interaction fit most naturally into the challenges of each Depth of Knowledge? Find out, chapter by chapter.

Aligning Rigor and the Reading-Writing Connection

Many schools and districts ask me to work with their teachers on "writing." I always need to ask, "Do you mean writing short answers to constructed-response questions, approximately a paragraph or two? Or do you mean writing full stories or analytical essays of many paragraphs, like arguments and informational pieces?" The challenges are different.

Connecting reading and writing by writing to sources is a new expectation for many learners, especially younger ones. How do reading and writing standards work together and how are they different at different Depths of Knowledge? More important, how do we support the reading-writing connection through our day-to-day instruction?

Aligning Rigor and Formative Assessment

Whether scoring reading or writing, we need to measure what our students have achieved so we know to what extent they (and we) have been successful. There are many kinds of assessments, but for classroom purposes, we will focus in this book on formative measures.

Formative assessment "refers to a wide variety of methods that teachers use to conduct in-process evaluations of student comprehension, learning needs, and academic progress during a lesson, unit, or course" (Glossary of Education Reform, 2014). In short, formative assessments seek to *inform* instruction, to answer the question: *Where shall I go next with my teaching?* We are trying to find out: *Did my students achieve the goal I intended? Who "gets it"? Who doesn't "get it"? Are there common problems among students who did not demonstrate sufficient understanding? What are the problems? Who needs reteaching? How will I reteach this?*

Assessing comprehension is tricky because "comprehension" can mean many things depending on the Depth of Knowledge we are measuring. Are we determining students' understanding of basic text *content*? Are we measuring their competence in applying a comprehension *skill*? Are we examining their *metacognition*, their ability to think strategically about what they read? Are we analyzing their capacity to *use* textual knowledge to synthesize sources and solve a problem?

For meaningful formative assessment, the monitoring task must measure the rigor of what we teach. So our first job is to know which Depth of Knowledge we want to evaluate and to determine the criteria by which that DOK should be analyzed. Hence, rubrics will be essential to using the data we collect to drive our instruction.

As we contemplate formative assessment, we should also consider how we can guide teachers in their instruction aimed at the rigor of each Depth of Knowledge. If you're a teacher, how can you reflect on your own practice to take the next step forward? If you're a coach, how can you support your colleagues' pursuit of best practices for each DOK in a nonevaluative way? If you're an administrator, what should you look and listen for when you visit classrooms to observe lessons or talk with teachers about comprehension instruction? The Protocol for Monitoring and Supporting Instruction for Deep Thinking on page 196 of Chapter 7 offers a starting point for professional reflection.

Mapping the Path Forward: The Rest of This Book

The Depths of Knowledge build on each other, so that in the end we maximize students' "sophisticated understanding of fundamental ideas"—rigor's gold standard. Here is how the rest of this book is organized, with the goal of supporting your efforts to help students achieve and demonstrate rigor in their literacy learning.

Part 1: The Depths of Knowledge in Literacy (Chapters 1–4)

In Part 1 of this book, we'll unpack the levels, beginning with DOK 1. Each topic in the list that follows is addressed sequentially in Chapters 1 through 4, as applied to DOK 1 through DOK 4, respectively:

- *Understanding Underlying Principles: The Rigor at Each Depth of Knowledge*—This is where understanding the rigor associated with each Depth of Knowledge begins. What kind of thinking will be expected of students?
- *Measuring Depth of Knowledge on Standards-Based Assessments*—Each chapter includes examples of questions for each Depth of Knowledge from released items and practice tests. Items are organized by standard and have been carefully researched to represent questions that appear on tests frequently.
- *Aligning Rigor and Standards*—After examining the items themselves, we will explore the challenges they pose, as well as hints for making the toughest items more manageable.
- *Aligning Rigor and Text Complexity*—For each Depth of Knowledge, we will identify the kind of complexity best suited to the rigor of that DOK. Also provided is a list of texts from the bibliography in Chapter 7 (Teaching Tools and Resources) that are well suited to that qualitative complexity.
- *Aligning Rigor and Close Reading*—Each chapter provides close reading guidelines appropriate to that Depth of Knowledge, as well as easy-to-implement classroom strategies. Tools for students to use during and after close reading for each DOK are included in Chapter 7.
- *Aligning Rigor and Student Interaction*—Different Depths of Knowledge call for different interactive strategies. These are explained in each chapter, along with classroom scenarios showing these strategies in action.
- *Aligning Rigor and the Reading-Writing Connection*—Students are now expected to write about their reading in different ways for different Depths of Knowledge. But write *what*? Find suggestions in each chapter to take back to your classroom.
- *Aligning Rigor and Formative Assessment*—There are many ways to assess students' thinking at each Depth of Knowledge, but one or more strategies will be highlighted and explained in every chapter as a place to begin. Rubrics for evaluating students' performance on each formative assessment are featured in Chapter 7.

Part 2: Materials to Support DOK in Literacy Instruction (Chapters 5–7)

In Part 2, we'll identify and provide resources for each Depth of Knowledge that are classroom-ready and can be used to streamline planning for literacy instruction and assessment. These resources include the following:

- *Sample Lessons and Planning Templates* (Chapter 5)—In this chapter, you will find a model lesson to support each Depth of Knowledge that can be used as a prototype for lessons you write yourself. A planning template follows each lesson for this purpose. Lesson components are explained step-by-step to support *your* lesson design.

- *Books and Other Resources That Inspire Deep Thinking* (Chapter 6)—What kinds of books and other resources will work best for inspiring rigor? In this chapter, you will find an annotated bibliography of short texts with a variety of qualitative complexities that will keep kids tuned in. These resources are integrated into different chapters and support different Depths of Knowledge.
- *Teaching Tools and Resources* (Chapter 7)—The final chapter contains classroom-ready tools and resources that support all Depths of Knowledge. These include anchor charts, rubrics, planning forms, graphic organizers, and more. An explanation is provided for how to use each resource most effectively.

Let the Learning Begin

Of course, the bibliographies provided in this book could have included thousands of other worthy titles; and for each Depth of Knowledge, there could have been more assessment items, instructional practices, and tools for teachers and students. But I shouldn't be the one having all the fun here! These resources, practices, and principles will give you a place to begin. Use these exemplars to design models and protocols of your own, just right for the students in your care. As you read, consider the following questions:

- *Teachers*—What can you use from this book "as is"—no modifications needed? What do you need to adapt or modify for your grade level? For high or low achievers? For students with special needs? For English learners? How will you make these revisions?
- *Coaches*—How will your enhanced understanding of rigor affect your work with colleagues? What can you model in classrooms? How else can you help teachers grow in their implementation of best practices that lead to rigor for their students?
- *Administrators*—What kinds of opportunities for discourse around rigor can you structure so that teachers learn to think systematically about what rigor means to students' thinking? How can you monitor the implementation of rigor-related practices schoolwide—or districtwide if you serve at that level?

And for all educators, there are "bottom line" summaries of key points throughout the text. Use these to reinforce your professional learning.

PART 1

The Depths of Knowledge in Literacy

1

Evidence: Supporting Depth of Knowledge 1

Depth of Knowledge 1 is the foundation for all of the other levels. Before we unpack this DOK to understand its relation to assessment items, standards, text complexity, close reading, student interaction, the reading-writing connection, and formative assessment, let's examine its underlying principles.

Underlying Principles: Rigor for DOK 1

According to Webb (2007), the rigor for readers at this first Depth of Knowledge is their precision in identifying specific textual evidence as they recall and reproduce information (see Figure 1.1). Tasks at this level require only a basic understanding—information that comes directly off the page, no interpretation needed. The response may be an exact word or words found within the text, or language that is very close. Do students have the right facts and details? Can they answer *who, what, when, where, why*, and *how*? The answer will be right or it will be wrong—no margin of error here. Students either know the answer or they don't. As applied to literacy, Level 1 of the Depths of Knowledge involves a one-step process: returning to the text to check for accuracy.

FIGURE 1.1 | Depth of Knowledge 1 and Rigor

Depth of Knowledge 1	The Rigor
Recalling and reproducing information	Precision in identifying the best textual evidence

Measuring DOK 1 on Standards-Based Assessments

New standards-based assessments will not include many reading items that focus exclusively on DOK 1. Rigor at Depth of Knowledge 1 is a component of all standards and of all subsequent Depths of Knowledge because all reading comprehension must be based on evidence.

The chart in Figure 1.2, which includes released items and items from practice tests, identifies questions like those students can expect to see on standards-based assessments. In addition to DOK 1 items for Reading (R), students will see a few Writing (W) items as well—not "real" writing like producing stories and essays, but multiple-choice questions that address spelling, grammar, usage, and writing mechanics. There will also be a few Language (L) items for students to demonstrate their editing skills.

FIGURE 1.2 | Sample Assessment Items for DOK 1

Standard	Focus	Sample Questions
R1: Evidence	Text evidence	Which detail in the text helps you understand _____?
R2: Development of Ideas	Development of ideas	What is the second step in the development of _____?
R3: Text Elements	Story parts/facts	Where does the story take place?
R4: Vocabulary	Determining word meaning	The author uses a word that means _____. Click on a word in the passage that is closest to that meaning.
R5: Text Structure	Understanding text structure	Which fact is found under [heading 2]?
R6: Purpose and Point of View	Purpose and point of view	Who is speaking in [paragraph 3]?
L2	Editing	Choose the sentence that contains a spelling error.
L2	Editing	Click on two words that should be followed by commas.
W-3.d	Precise language	Choose two words that best replace the underlined words for clarity and tone.

Aligning Rigor and Standards for DOK 1

We need only look as far as Standard 1 of Common Core's College and Career Readiness Anchor Standards for Reading to see that this is the standard we should focus on for the rigor of Depth of Knowledge 1:

1. Read closely to determine what the text says explicitly and to make logical inferences from it; cite specific textual evidence when writing or speaking to support conclusions drawn from the text. (http://www.corestandards.org/assets/CCSSI_ELA%20Standards.pdf)

In fact, this standard identifies itself as the "close reading" and "evidence" standard, the standard that focuses on determining what the text says explicitly, citing specific textual evidence, or perhaps deriving a few basic inferences. Although most evidence for Depth of Knowledge 1 will be aligned with Reading Standard 1, a few evidence questions may fall under other standards. Some of the sample assessment items in the chart in Figure 1.2 reflect this.

Regardless of the designated standard, the expectation is clear: it's all about the evidence—finding it, citing it, and responding to questions about it orally and in writing. As we select texts, scaffold instruction, and plan for formative assessment, we need to think about best practices in these areas that will provide students with the evidence base they need not only to achieve the rigor of Depth of Knowledge 1, but also to form the foundation needed for rigor at deeper Depths of Knowledge.

The Format of DOK 1 Items

If you examine sample assessment items on sites such as the SBAC portal or PARCC online, you will see that these questions appear as multiple-choice (also called "selected response") items. Common Core Reading Standard 1, essentially the "evidence standard," is often listed along with another standard aligned with the item. Why? Although the item might be aimed primarily at students' knowledge of the author's purpose or theme or character traits, students must prove their response with *evidence*.

You will also find that Part B of two-part questions addresses evidence. For example, Part A might ask the question: *What is the meaning of [calamity] as it is used in paragraph 2?* Part B will push for validation: *What clue in the text helped you understand the meaning of [calamity]?*

In the classroom, for instructional purposes, questions with single right/wrong answers may be oral or written, but we should try to make response *authentic*. In our life as "real" readers, we are seldom given four options from which to choose, so let's not reduce literacy to "bubbling in" as we study great literature and informational text with our students. For oral or written response, however, students will need a large fund of words to express their knowledge of the evidence—which brings us to the need for academic language.

Academic Language and Visual Support for DOK 1

Much of the academic language students need will not be restricted to DOK 1. But this is where our work with words must begin so students can enjoy an efficient command of literary vocabulary within all Depths of Knowledge.

The first academic vocabulary challenge students face at any Depth of Knowledge is the need for an understanding of the concepts upon which literary thinking is built. Without knowing the meaning behind the words that they see in test items, how will they know which evidence is the right evidence? Do they know the meaning of terms like *character trait, theme, motivation,* and hundreds more academic terms they will encounter? And then, can they label different themes, traits, and motivations using precise language? They'll need this knowledge so they can choose the right option when they answer those multiple-choice questions. For example, what do we mean by "character motivation" and what might motivate a character? We need to teach these concepts, but then we need to make them visible so students can reference them easily.

Visions of anchor charts dance in my head! I see lists of literary terms, possible themes, character traits and feelings, motivations, attitudes, problems, and more. For ease of access, these are provided in Figures 7.14 through 7.20 on pages 177–183.

Where to Increase Instructional Focus for DOK 1

In recent years, there has been so much emphasis on the need for deep thinking that teachers have become almost reluctant to spend much time on questions that ask only for evidence. I think that's the wrong approach.

Asking straightforward evidence questions is a valuable way to monitor meaning and basic comprehension. Too often teachers go immediately to higher-level tasks that assume entry-level knowledge—like "Do you think there's more evidence for the existence of the Loch Ness Monster or the Yeti?" When students can't respond, it's their lack of higher-level thinking ability that is presumed the culprit.

But truth to tell, if the teacher had asked a very rudimentary question first—"What is the evidence that the Loch Ness Monster exists?"—it would have been clear that the real problem lay in lack of foundational understanding. **The problem with DOK 1 questions is not that we shouldn't ask them, but that we shouldn't stop there.** When you ask a basic evidence question, you can follow up by digging deeper.

Monitor students' understanding of DOK 1 during close reading by asking questions such as these: "What information or details did the author provide on this page or in this paragraph?" "What do you know now that you didn't know before?" Follow up with more specific questions related to other standards and Depths of Knowledge: "Based on the details on this page, what *caused* this problem?" (DOK 2; Standard 3). Support younger students or students who struggle with language by asking them to draw a picture of their Level 1 knowledge, showing accurate and thorough details.

Follow any question with an expectation that students will return to the text to support their claim with evidence: "How do you know?" We should see eyes dropping to the page, scanning line by line, and perhaps fingers flipping between pages. "Right here!" we want them to say. "Right here is the proof."

> **Bottom Line for Aligning Rigor and Standards for DOK 1:** The standard that should receive the strongest emphasis for Depth of Knowledge 1 is College and Career Readiness Anchor Standard for Reading 1. The language within this standard—*closely, explicitly, logical*—will keep us focused on what matters most for the rigor of this Depth of Knowledge.

Aligning Rigor and Text Complexity for DOK 1

There are times when we cannot choose our instructional resources. Maybe we are obliged to use a core program with reading selections predetermined, or maybe our science or social studies unit requires a specific text or topics. But almost all of us have a little wiggle room somewhere within our school day for a piece of literature or an informational source that kids will enjoy.

Perhaps there's a book or a short story that connects to a required text. If we're extra lucky, the text might even be a part of the grade-level curriculum. Either way, if students are intrigued by the content, they'll more readily tune in to the details. Hence, we need complex texts that not only meet the qualitative and quantitative criteria identified by the Common Core but also interest readers.

Texts That Intrigue Students

What kind of texts do students find intriguing? For starters, texts about animals—the more unique, the better. Some animals seem to have almost universal appeal: pandas, sea turtles, sharks, and platypuses, to name a few. I have an adorable book I love to read to primary students, *Panda Kindergarten*, by Joanne Ryder. It's a true account of panda cubs raised together at the Wolong Nature Preserve in China, where they learn skills that prepare them to be released into the wild. It's an endearing story. But it's the beautiful photographs that captivate young children and make the facts memorable. Don't forget the power of illustrations to make details come alive.

Also in the primary grades, there's the lure of those ancient beasts, dinosaurs, and at many grade levels, monsters real or imagined, like the Loch Ness Monster and Bigfoot. Recently I had an especially scintillating experience with rats. I was asked to model a close reading lesson in a middle school classroom during the last period of the day on a muggy Friday afternoon in late September.

Almost all of us have a little wiggle room somewhere within our school day for a piece of literature or an informational source that kids will enjoy.

I decided to use a passage from the book *Oh, Rats!: The Story of Rats and People* by Albert Marrin. It was my first time using this text, so I couldn't gauge the appeal. However, I did hope for reasonable engagement because a large audience of teachers would be observing the lesson.

I needn't have worried. Turns out this book met one of the key criteria by which middle schoolers evaluate great literature: it was gross. I read aloud, "In the United States, the Department of Agriculture estimates that rats spoil over 400,000 tons of food a year with their urine and droppings."

"Eeww," the class chorused in unison with each additional nauseating fact. And hands waved wildly every time I checked for understanding. Even as the dismissal bell rang, the students begged me to read another paragraph or two. A month later when I returned, they were still asking for the "rat book." It appeared that those rodents had gnawed their way straight into kids' long-term memory, so accurate was their recall of the details they had read.

Intermediate-grade students respond well to humor. They get hooked by a few funny lines and then get absorbed in the merit of the work, which often extends beyond a few chuckles. A favorite in this category is *Because of Mr. Terupt*, by Rob Buyea. This story of a new 5th grade teacher is told through the lens of seven students in his class, all of whom will resonate with the "tween" crowd. The book begins with this sentence: "It's our bad luck to have teachers in this world, but since we're stuck with them, the best we can do is hope to get a brand-new one instead of a mean old fart." With that opener, you have every-one's attention immediately. Meanwhile, embedded in those comedic sentences are pearls of wisdom about thinking for yourself. While students are remember-ing the funny parts, they're also reflecting on the details that made the events so poignant.

Other things students like to learn about are remarkable achievements, especially those accomplished by children near their own age. Did someone survive challenging circumstances? That gets students' attention. Was risk involved? They like action, danger, and daring, as well as mystery, science fiction, and sports.

Intriguing Texts to Get Started

The books included in the following list (cited with complete references in Chapter 6, Books and Other Resources That Inspire Deep Thinking) offer the kind of intriguing content that will keep kids tuned in to evidence. Of course, other texts from this bibliography may also be highly engaging, and don't forget your personal favorites.

Texts that will intrigue grades K–2 students

- "The New Kid on the Block," by Jack Prelutsky—There's plenty of evi-dence about this bully—what students *think* they know. Until the last line. Reread this poem to see where your thinking might have gone off track.

- *Stand Tall, Molly Lou Mellon*, **by Patty Lovell**—Can Molly Lou survive the nastiness of Ronald Durkin? Will Ronald get his comeuppance? Keep reading to see how this primary page-turner turns out.
- *Down the Road*, **by Alice Schertle**—It will be obvious to children that Hetty is making some bad choices after earning the privilege of going to the store all by herself. How will Hetty's parents deal with her bad behavior? Were you surprised by the ending?

Texts that will intrigue grades 3–5 students

- *The Can Man*, **by Laura Williams**—Will Tim get the skateboard he's been saving to buy? Will the Can Man get his much-needed winter coat? The suspense in this book keeps readers tuned in. The sweet ending comes as a surprise.
- "Spaghetti," **by Cynthia Rylant**—This short story has so many loose ends that the reader will want to keep going just to find answers to some of those unanswered questions.
- *A Tale of Segregation: Fetching Water* **(ReadWorks)**—Could this incident actually have happened? The outrage will keep students reading to see how this brief account is resolved.

Texts that will intrigue grades 6-8 students

- *My Secret Camera: Life in a Lodz Ghetto*, **photographs by Mendel Grossman; text by Frank Dabba Smith**—Middle school students will be aghast—but mesmerized—by this photo journal depicting the atrocities of life in a Nazi work camp.
- *Japanese Internment Camps: A Personal Account* **(ReadWorks); "In Response to Executive Order 9066," by Dwight Okita (poem)**—This article and this poem continue the theme of incredulity that such discrimination and persecution could have ever played a role in history—this time within the United States.
- *Oh, Rats! The Story of Rats and People*, **by Albert Marrin**—Students can't get enough of the gross details—and the strange notion that rats might even be *helpful* in some regards.

> **Bottom Line for Aligning Rigor and Text Complexity for DOK 1:** Choosing texts that students find intriguing will go far in encouraging them to *want* to find evidence, and in helping the evidence *stick.*

Aligning Rigor and Close Reading for DOK 1

In the end, the reason we teach to the rigor of any Depth of Knowledge is not so students can do well on a test (though we wouldn't object if this was a consequence of our good teaching), but so students can move toward that "sophisticated level of understanding" that marks a great thinker. What close reading instructional practices can contribute to students' achievement of the DOK 1 rigor, precision in identifying specific evidence? Consider these possibilities:

- *Before reading:* Support students by minimizing frontloading.
- *During reading:* Support students by promoting independent close reading and asking text-dependent questions that require rereading.
- *After reading:* Support students by teaching the art of rereading.

Before Reading: Support Students by Minimizing Frontloading

The part of literacy instruction known as "prereading"—the part of the lesson that takes place before students read the text—has been the source of much controversy since the inception of the Common Core. Lead authors David Coleman and Susan Pimentel (2012), received a lot of pushback for this instructional guideline:

> Scaffolding should not preempt or replace the text by translating its contents for students or telling students what they are going to learn in advance of reading the text; the scaffolding should not become an alternate, simpler source of information that diminishes the need for students to read the text itself carefully.

Many educators viewed this statement as demolishing the long-held belief that students need extensive scaffolding before reading to maximize their comprehension. "What about English learners?" teachers cried. "What about my struggling readers?"

Prereading scaffolding was well intentioned, and of course teachers should support students who are unprepared to manage the demands of the texts they read. Such students might include English learners or other students with language or other needs. But this lesson component has gotten a little out of hand. How many students are we scaffolding who, in fact, *could* read the text without all that help from us if given the chance? Are we teaching in a way that fosters independence or dependence? And more important, what should instruction that places more of this prereading responsibility on students look like?

Classroom scenario: Scaffolding students before reading

Let's visit a classroom of the past where a 2nd grade teacher is getting ready to read her students a picture book about Abraham Lincoln, *Abe Lincoln: The Boy Who Loved Books*, by Kay Winters. The teacher asks students what they know about Abe, some of which is true and some of which is not. She corrects their misinformation (Lincoln didn't fight in the Revolutionary War; he wasn't friends with Martin Luther King Jr.).

She asks what they think the book might be about. Kids like to speculate and are eager to make predictions: "He might get killed." "He might help a slave." "He might have a beard." These guesses continue unchecked, though they don't quite match the subtitle (*The Boy Who Loved Books*), nor the cover illustration showing young Abe reading a book high up in the limbs of a tree.

But the "beard" prediction triggers some personal connections: "My uncle has a beard." "I don't like my dad's beard." How did we float off into this netherworld of beards when we were supposed to be thinking about Abraham Lincoln? Superficial personal connections have a way of inserting themselves into potentially powerful conversations, whether we've asked for connections or not.

This teacher brings everyone's attention back to the text as her smartboard springs to life, revealing a half-dozen vocabulary words from the book that she defines and explains. The clock says 10 o'clock. Twenty minutes have ticked by since this lesson began. "We'll save the book for tomorrow," the teacher announces. "It's time for guided reading."

If our goal is for students to find evidence, we might want to rethink what happened in this lesson: eliciting prior knowledge, those pesky personal connections, and vocabulary frontloading. This was a nice general discussion about Abraham Lincoln, but it didn't necessarily prepare students to read *this* book about him.

A new vision for scaffolding before reading

As you plan any lesson, read the text beforehand and ask yourself this question: Does the author build the knowledge needed to understand the content *within* the text, or does she make some assumptions that will derail students' understanding without clarification up front? I think you will find that most authors *do* build the needed concepts right into their book; that's the point of the book. So let the student and the author take control of this. It's the author's job to make the meaning clear. It's the student's job to find the evidence that supports the meaning.

There will be little need for close reading if the teacher has offered up the spoiler alert before the reading begins. But if we're not going to do all this frontloading, what *should* we do to make sure students get the evidence they need? We should get them to notice helpful hints on the cover of a book or in the layout of the text so they can learn to support themselves as strategic readers: "What are the important words in the title?" "What details do you think the illustrator wanted us to notice?" If the source is not a book but an article or something else, are there other text features available, like headings or bolded words to note before diving into the text itself? The point isn't to use these observations to make predictions, but for students to recognize as they read how a word in the title or a detail in the illustration comes to bear on the author's meaning.

It's the author's job to make the meaning clear. It's the student's job to find the evidence that supports the meaning.

And the best part is this: noticing these clues to meaning takes only about two to three minutes. This gives students more time *in* the text.

During Reading: Support Students by Promoting Independent Close Reading and Asking Text-Dependent Questions That Require Rereading

Support for students during reading includes careful monitoring of their independent close reading and asking text-dependent questions (TDQs) that will require them to reread the text.

Independent close reading

Students should be poised to embark on the close reading of an article or other short text after brief guidance to get started. The evidence they need is right in front of them. And you can make sure they find all of it by posing a few well-positioned text-dependent questions. But who do we want to be in charge here? If *we* ask those TDQs, then *we* are leading the learning. How can we transfer some of this responsibility to students so *they* are in charge?

I propose a simple solution. It is unrealistic to expect students to ask the kinds of specific questions we create for the many fine points of a text: "Who was full of bluster, the North Wind or the Sun?" "When did the Traveler unfasten his cloak?" However, students can ask themselves one or two basic questions, and they can ask them often: "What are the details the author is giving me in this part of the text?" "Are there any words I need to clarify?"

When students closely read a text for the first time, they are not reading to meet an isolated objective like identifying character traits or a theme, but to retrieve as much evidence as possible from which to construct meaning about the text in general: What is this story, article, or poem about? This is not reading for the gist. The gist is an overall impression, the one big idea that emerges from a text. It's fine for students to read a text initially from beginning to end simply to get this big idea if you'd like them to do so. But this is not what we mean by "close reading," and reading for the gist is not going to yield much evidence.

Monitoring by noting important details

To get the evidence, invite students to respond to this question: "What details am I getting in this part of the text?" Pausing frequently to ponder this question will not only help students retrieve evidence but also allow them to monitor their comprehension as well: "Do I understand what I am reading? Or am I a little lost?"

If students are reading on their own, annotating the text will support their accountability. They can mark the text itself if that is an option. If not, you can provide an annotation sheet such as one of those provided in Chapter 7. See Figure 7.5: Finding Evidence as I Read Literature (page 166) and Figure 7.6: Finding Evidence as I Read Information (page 167).

> There will be little need for close reading if the teacher has offered up the spoiler alert before the reading begins.

If students are reading the text with the teacher and some peers in a small group, this monitoring can be done orally. Pause and ask, "What details did you find right here, in this paragraph?" I love this scenario because it's so authentic. This is what good readers do as they read—stop and reflect on what the author has told them so far, and go back to reread if that meaning seems fuzzy.

The success of this stop-and-reflect strategy will depend on one key factor: the amount of text students read each time before they pause. In so many classroom lessons I've observed, the teacher waited until students had read the entire short story, poem, or article before checking for comprehension. It was no surprise that many students struggled with citing even basic evidence because their comprehension was probably off track from the start.

For most elementary students, new to the expectations of independent close reading, and even lots of middle school students, you will want to read short chunks of text, probably a single stanza or paragraph, or maybe two, before stopping to reflect. When I supply students with a duplicated page with a poem or a brief article, I physically draw lines under the paragraphs where I want them to pause. Teaching students to determine their own pausing points is a great next step, as it signals even more independence.

Monitoring by noting words that need clarification

What about those words that need clarification? Determining the meaning of words from context is more of a DOK 2 expectation than a DOK 1 issue, and it will be addressed in the next chapter. However, identifying words that warrant clarification is well suited to this first Depth of Knowledge. I like the idea of asking students to locate words that are new to them or that they can't easily define or use. This gives lack of word knowledge a new status. Rather than being ashamed of a word they don't comprehend, they are instead congratulated for finding the word and recognizing that they need to understand it more deeply. When they pause after each chunk, ask them to find those words!

It's easy to know whether these strategies for independent close reading are working because if they are, students will be able to talk about the evidence they found. Note that this approach to independent close reading does not place a great deal of emphasis on annotating the text. Over the last few years, I've noticed that annotation has become almost synonymous with close reading; as long as students are marking up their text, they are reading closely.

But too often, this seems to move the focus from comprehension to coding. If students feel inspired to jot a note here and there, that's great. I'm a big text-annotator myself and know how valuable this personalization can be. Let's not attempt to legislate this behavior, however. When I see line after line highlighted in yellow, or many minutes devoted to crafting sticky-note messages, I wonder if the time might have been better spent *thinking* about the reading and responding later. With or without annotation, you'll most likely need a few TDQs in your back pocket to check for understanding.

Posing text-dependent questions that require rereading

Even when you begin by asking students to find the evidence themselves, it's likely they'll miss a few of the fine points (and maybe some of the major ones, too). You'll want to know the text well enough yourself so you can follow up after each chunk with TDQs that zoom in on the details they've overlooked.

Most of the questions on the new assessments designed only to elicit evidence will be specific to the text, not prototype items that could be asked regarding other passages as well. Within your instruction, DOK 1 questions will be specific to the text too. Deciding what to ask for this basic evidence won't be difficult because these are the same kinds of questions we've been asking forever, typically beginning with one of those "5W/H" words. Remember for this Depth of Knowledge that the answer should be *stated* and in plain view within the text—though it should involve careful looking. Here are some examples:

- *Who* started the skirmish between the Redcoats and the Patriots during the Boston Massacre?
- *What* were the Wolf's exact words when he said he would blow down the First Little Pig's house?
- *Where* did the Civil War officially begin?
- *When* do you add the sugar to the recipe?
- *Why* were mammoths able to survive such cold weather, according to the information in paragraph 2?
- Which sentence on this page lets us know *how* Tom Sawyer got his friends to paint the picket fence?

The answers to these questions would be easy—*if* students returned to the text to verify their response. Yes, these are basic evidence questions. But no, you might be surprised that they are not quite "no-brainers." There are nuances and small points that can be confusing without a closer look.

Better return to that paragraph about the Patriot/Redcoat skirmish during the Boston Massacre to see who was responsible for initiating the fight. Do you add the sugar to that recipe before or after the eggs? Reread to find out. At first glance, these may seem like inconsequential details, though down the line, that basic knowledge may play a larger role in applying a skill or making an inference.

After Reading: Support Students by Teaching the Art of Rereading

There will be plenty of times when we ask great text-dependent questions for which students don't give us the right answer—or any answer. They avoid eye contact. They fumble through a few words before saying they "don't remember," or they stare at the ceiling as if it's a jumbotron, hoping the right words will magically appear there in neon lights. We rephrase the question or call on another student, but still… nothing.

This is our cue to send them back to the text, to *reread* so they can produce the evidence needed to answer the question. Unfortunately, this is more complicated than it would appear. Some students, even big ones, don't have a clear idea how to approach rereading. Their strategy, if we can call it that, is to go back to the beginning of the article or the first page of whatever they are reading and "take it from the top." We need to show them that there's a more efficient way. We can model this in the context of our current lesson:

> Let's think about this. We want to find out which animals are predators of panda cubs. If I was rereading this article to locate that information, I'd first check the headings: Panda Habitats; Pandas' Natural Enemies and Defenses; Pandas' Diet. I know that a predator is an enemy, so I'll reread the information in this section first.

We can then demonstrate how we check for evidence sentence by sentence:

> The first sentence in this section doesn't help me, but look at the second sentence: "Potential predators include jackals, snow leopards and yellow-throated martens, all of which are capable of killing and eating panda cubs." Success! This is exactly what I was looking for, and it just took me a few seconds to find it.

Students dread rereading because they assume they'll be at it forever and with no certainty of success. But it doesn't have to be this way. Show them there's an "art" to rereading, and once they get good at it, it's quick and easy.

Another approach to the art of rereading is to teach it as a minilesson. Separated from the stress of producing an on-the-spot answer to something they missed in the first round, everyone can now relax and approach the quest calmly. Offer up some hypothetical examples:

> Suppose we wanted evidence about what counteracts gravity. How would we know what part of this chapter to reread? Yes, *counteracts* is in bold print under the second heading. Let's look under that heading first.

> What if we wanted details about the life cycle of frogs? Ah, that information is in the text box rather than in the main text.

We spend lots of time teaching students the purpose of various text features, but more hands-on practice with *using* those features would benefit students as they're rereading informational sources.

What about rereading when the text is literary? This isn't as simple, but it's still doable. Consider this example:

> Are you looking for information about a certain character? Do a quick scan of the pages you read to locate that character's name. Now read that section more closely to see if the information you need is there. Are you looking for a specific line of dialogue? Scan for words inside quotation marks.

Whatever they're looking for, teach students that a systematic approach works best when they need to find something quickly.

> **Bottom Line for Aligning Rigor and Close Reading for DOK 1:**
> Before close reading, try not to do too much of the work for students, so they must *read* to get the evidence. Teach strategies so students can support themselves. Independent close reading can be an effective means of getting students to retrieve evidence and unknown words on their own, and it should be the first line of defense before falling back on teacher-led, text-dependent questions.
>
> But regardless of how competent your students are with independent close reading, you may want to supplement their initial construction of meaning with a few carefully selected text-dependent questions before moving forward with tasks that probe deeper thinking—just to make sure they're ready. Remember that students may be reluctant to reread not just because they don't like to do it, but also because they don't know how to do it efficiently. You can change that with modeling or mini-lessons that demonstrate *how*.

Aligning Rigor and Student Interaction for DOK 1

Active reading is not always a matter of discussion. In fact, for the rigor of DOK 1, active reading probably won't yield much conversation because student responses are restricted to evidence—which is typically right or wrong and not open to debate. In addition to responding directly to a question, interaction for DOK 1 can mean opportunities such as thumbs up/thumbs down, choral response, and restating.

Approaches to active reading will vary at different grade ranges. I once watched a 1st grade teacher keep her students actively engaged and interactive using I Spy cards (see Figure 7.1 in Chapter 7, page 159). She printed out several sheets of these cards on cardstock, cut the cards apart, and had a hefty stack of them next to her as she conducted a close reading lesson of a picture book. Pausing after each page, she asked, "Who can tell me a detail the author shared with us on this page?" When someone offered a nicely paraphrased detail, the teacher rewarded that student with an I Spy card. I noticed that the teacher was selective in handing out these cards; they were only awarded for specific evidence that was clearly stated in complete sentences. I also noticed that students were proud to receive the cards: "I got three." "I got four." They may or may not have realized that "winning" was more about comprehension than collecting cards.

In the intermediate grades, students like to respond chorally if they have their own copy of the text: "Find the sentence in paragraph 1 that describes the appearance of the main character. Ready… set… go!" I allow a few seconds for students to find the correct evidence, and then they read it aloud in unison.

Also with older students, I often ask more than one for the same basic answer, without waiting for raised hands: "What is the capital of Illinois?" Yes, the first student who responded gave me the correct answer, but do other students know the answer as well? And are they paying attention or lost in their own thoughts? Sometimes I switch it up fast: "The capital of Illinois?" "The capital of North Dakota?" "The capital of West Virginia?" This keeps everyone on their toes because no one wants to be caught unawares with the eyes of their peers all turned in their direction.

> **Bottom Line for Aligning Rigor and Student Interaction for DOK 1:** We need to find a way to promote active and interactive reading in all grades. When students are actively on task and held accountable, there is greater likelihood that they will identify evidence accurately.

Aligning Rigor and the Reading-Writing Connection for DOK 1

Aligning reading and writing to the rigor of Depth of Knowledge 1 is clear cut. Select the answer (or answers) you want from among several multiple-choice options. For online assessments, the item might ask instead to click on the correct words or part of the sentence. Getting the answer right, however, will require the same thing every time: spot-on accuracy. We can achieve this precision in the classroom, and we can do it authentically. We can hold students accountable to high expectations.

High Expectations in Action

Quality evidence is specific, not general. It *shows* instead of *tells*. Here's the difference. I had done a close reading of the picture book *More Than Anything Else*, by Marie Bradby, with a class of 4th graders. The book is about Booker T. Washington and his desire to learn to read "more than anything else." At the end of the story, we decided that one character trait that Booker exhibited throughout his childhood was *persistence*. I then asked students to write a response with one carefully chosen piece of evidence from the text in support of this character trait. That was all. Just find the evidence, a DOK 1 expectation. I didn't even push for an explanation—a natural extension, but more aligned to deeper thinking.

The first student wrote, "Booker was persistent in learning to read because he never gave up. He kept trying." This is generally correct but could apply to anyone who was persistent. The second student defended this trait by saying, "Booker asked the newspaper man." Asked him what? How could you link this event to persistence? A third student offered this: "Booker was persistent because even when he came home and was in pain from a whole day working in the salt mines, he still kept trying to figure out words." What a great answer! This third student chose a specific detail from the story and tied it to persistence.

Now what do we do with Students 1 and 2 to transform their answer from not-quite-there to goal? Begin with immediate and honest feedback while the task is still fresh in their mind and they haven't mentally moved on to another assignment (or the anticipation of recess). Next, expect accuracy—because you know the students can read this book and are capable of rising to this challenge: "Find a page where Booker is showing persistence. Then in your answer describe exactly what is happening. Find a quote, or put it into your own words." It may take a couple of tries, but hold out for evidence that is specific. And hope that the next time an assignment calls for evidence, these students will demonstrate a little persistence of their own.

It is true that evidence alone is a low-level indicator of comprehension. But it is also true that without solid evidence and an understanding of why we selected *this* piece of evidence, we have no path forward to deeper thinking. The same holds true for linking reading to the writing standards.

Connecting to the Writing Standards

The "writing" that is assessed for DOK 1 relates only to editing: Is the word spelled right? Is the grammar correct? Does the subject agree with the verb? Does the syntax make sense?

There will probably be more of these kinds of "writing" items than those that assess students' recognition of writing that is well organized and well developed, or writing they produce themselves that demonstrates the qualities of good writing. But that does not mean students will find these questions easy. Could your 5th graders easily respond to the following assessment item?

Choose the sentence that is punctuated correctly.

A. You will be happy to learn Ms. Smith, that you have won the contest.
B. You will be happy to learn, Ms. Smith that you have won the contest.
C. You, will be happy to learn Ms. Smith, that you have won the contest.
D. You will be happy to learn, Ms. Smith, that you have won the contest.

Source: Sample grade 5 Writing question from https://portal
.smarterbalanced.org/library/en/grade-5-ela-practice-test-scoring-guide.pdf

> It is true that evidence alone is a low-level indicator of comprehension. But it is also true that without solid evidence and an understanding of why we selected *this* piece of evidence, we have no path forward to deeper thinking.

We should not forget that students' capacity to use conventions well is essential to good writing and should be a component of any writing curriculum.

> **Bottom Line for Aligning Rigor and Reading-Writing Connections for DOK 1:** Expect and insist upon accuracy with any literacy task that requires evidence, regardless of how basic the task may be. Hint: *Every* literacy task now requires evidence because teaching to new standards means students will always be responding to *sources.*

Aligning Rigor and Formative Assessment for DOK 1

Depth of Knowledge 1 is about understanding the basic content of a text, so the purpose of formative assessment at this level should be to measure how well students have retrieved the evidence related to content knowledge. To assess students formatively for the rigor of Depth of Knowledge 1, we can ask the same kinds of specific text-based questions they'll be asked on standards-based assessments. There will always be a place for checking understanding of text details, one at a time. But it's also important for students to recognize that comprehension is more than the accurate identification of a handful of random textual facts. How do these facts "add up"? How do they lead to meaning?

Assessing the Construction of Meaning

To assess the construction of meaning after an initial close reading, I propose a task that focuses on words and details—not defining hard words, which would be more of a DOK 2 task, but choosing the important words and the important details. What words and details stand out as essential to comprehending and talking about a text? Throughout their reading, students should be taking note of these important words: names, places, dates, words that are repeated, or words associated with a problem or a solution. They should be tuning in to story parts in narrative texts and facts in informational sources. The goal for after reading is to create a list that is not exhaustive, but selective.

We want students to choose their words and details carefully because the second part of this task is to explain *why* each word or detail is included on their list. A graphic organizer for this, Figure 7.7: Identifying Important Words and Details After Reading, is provided on page 168 in Chapter 7, and it could also be used as a formative assessment. Figure 1.3, page 34, illustrates how this graphic organizer might be completed by a student for the story *Cinderella.*

FIGURE 1.3 | Examples of Identifying Important Words and Details After Reading

This word in the text is important . . .	because . . .
1. Cinderella	She is the main character.
2. fairy godmother	She helps Cinderella.
3. stepsisters	They are mean to Cinderella.
4. prince	He saves Cinderella from misery.
5. glass slipper	This is how the problem gets solved.
6. midnight	This is the time when Cinderella was warned to leave the ball.
This detail in the text is important . . .	because . . .
1. Cinderella wants to go to the ball.	This gets the problem going.
2. The fairy godmother helps Cinderella.	The fairy godmother tried to solve Cinderella's problem.
3. Cinderella forgets to come home by midnight.	The problem is getting worse.
4. The glass slipper fits Cinderella.	This leads to the happy ending.

Navigating the Formative Assessment Task

A few things are notable about the task illustrated in Figure 1.3. First, the number of words designated is arbitrary and can be modified based on the length of the text and the skill of your students. Students enjoy this task and often beg to include additional words: "There are two more words I really, really need. Can I put them on my list? I can explain why they're so important." I agree to one or two extra words, but not five or six. The point here is to be *picky*.

Second, note that in a story the significant details can be defined by how they drive the problem and the solution to the problem. For informational text, aim for facts or details listed in order as this will support deeper comprehension like cause and effect and inferential thinking at other Depths of Knowledge.

Bottom Line for Aligning Rigor and Formative Assessments for DOK 1: In reading, formative assessment for Depth of Knowledge 1 is intended to examine students' understanding of basic textual content. This can be achieved with direct questions about the evidence in a text or with a generic task such as *identifying important words and details*, in which students choose the words and details they consider most essential to a text's general meaning.

2

Skills and Concepts: Supporting Depth of Knowledge 2

Building on the precision in identifying textual evidence that constitutes the rigor associated with the first Depth of Knowledge, DOK 2 requires students to apply skills and concepts accurately—and independently. (See Figure 2.1.) Let's begin our examination of this DOK by considering its underlying principles.

FIGURE 2.1 | **Depth of Knowledge 2 and Rigor**

Depth of Knowledge 2	The Rigor
Applying skills or knowledge of concepts	Independence in applying literacy skills and concepts accurately

Underlying Principles: Rigor for DOK 2

Just like the rigor of DOK 1, tasks at this level tend to have a single right answer. The difference at this depth, compared to DOK 1, is that the answer might be stated differently by different students. There is a process for deciding *how* to answer. Students must determine for themselves how to approach the task. Suppose the question asks for a summary, for example. Student A and Student B may write that summary a little differently. But in the end, an accurate summary contains about the same information.

DOK 2: Where the Application of Literacy Learning Begins

Although we can't deny the significance of DOK 1, the retrieval of evidence, as the cornerstone of literacy learning, the real *work* of reading begins at this second Depth of Knowledge, where students are tasked with *applying* skills and concepts. Preparing students for the rigor of DOK 2 means that we must have a solid grasp of which skills to teach and how to teach those skills well. We must also make sure that students understand the *concept* upon which a skill is based.

We teachers are not surprised by the need to teach skills. Reading skills have long been the stronghold of the literacy curriculum. Historically, the focus in the early grades has been mainly on foundational skills: phonological awareness, phonics, and fluency, with a little attention to comprehension as time allows. No one is quarreling with the need for these early literacy skills. But based on new standards, we also need a greater emphasis on comprehension from the primary grades onward—and we know from well-respected experts that this instruction should be explicit and systematic (Archer & Hughes, 2011).

We cannot wait for the intermediate grades to get serious about comprehension because students will have missed too much already. For confirmation, just look at the anchor standards and grade-level benchmarks for the Common Core's College and Career Readiness Standards. You will see that the same standards measured in middle school and beyond are the very ones identified as early as kindergarten. The expectations become more rigorous grade to grade, but consistent principles prevail across all grades.

Anchor Standards and Grade-Level Benchmarks

Here's the expectation for College and Career Readiness Anchor Standard 2 for Reading (http://www.corestandards.org/ELA-Literacy/CCRA/R/#CCSS .ELA-Literacy.CCRA.R.2):

> CCSS.ELA-LITERACY.CCRA.R.2: Determine central ideas or themes of a text and analyze their development; summarize the key supporting details and ideas.

Now look at the benchmark for this standard at three grade levels for informational text (http://www.corestandards.org/ELA-Literacy/):

> **Grade 1:** CCSS.ELA-LITERACY.RI.1.2: Identify the main topic and retell key details of a text.

> **Grade 4:** CCSS.ELA-LITERACY.RI.4.2: Determine the main idea of a text and explain how it is supported by key details; summarize the text.

> **Grade 7:** CCSS.ELA-LITERACY.RI.7.2: Determine two or more central ideas in a text and analyze their development over the course of the text; provide an objective summary of the text.

Identifying a central idea is a skill. At an early primary level, the expectation is simply to recognize the main *topic* and supporting details. By grade 4, students need to explain how the details are connected to the main *idea* in order to write a summary. Fast-forward to grade 7, where students must now identify *multiple* main ideas (or central ideas), analyze how the author developed them, and then use that understanding to create a summary.

Teachers often ask me if some comprehension standards are more critical than others in different grades. The short answer is no! No, because every standard has a grade-level benchmark that is appropriate to students at that level. I sometimes hear pushback about anchor standards and benchmarks that are "too hard" or "developmentally inappropriate." I disagree. *If* teachers understand the nuances of each standard, and *if* they embrace the related instruction knowledgeably, students can demonstrate the intended rigor.

To feel more comfortable with current expectations for comprehension skills, we first need a clear vision of what this rigor looks like on new assessments for Depth of Knowledge 2: What will students be expected to demonstrate for each standard? Let's begin by looking at how new assessments typically measure DOK 2.

Measuring DOK 2 on Standards-Based Assessments

New standards-based assessments will include lots of items that measure students' competence at this Depth of Knowledge. These will most likely be multiple-choice items, but they could also require a constructed response. There will be roughly the same number of DOK 2 (skills) items as DOK 3 (reasoning) items. This development changes the expectations for teachers and students considerably, because in the past, competence with comprehension *skills* was the main goal of literacy assessment (remember that RAND study mentioned in the Introduction) and hence was the main goal of literacy instruction.

We should not assume that our past practice in the teaching of skills will be sufficient for guiding students toward excellence on new assessments even at this second Depth of Knowledge. Figure 2.2 shows some examples (taken from released items and practice tests) of the kinds of questions students will be asked, aligned to Common Core reading comprehension and writing standards.

Aligning Rigor and Standards for DOK 2

If you're happy-dancing over these question stems, gleeful that you now know exactly what to ask your students so they'll be prepared for Depth of Knowledge 2 on state assessments, you may be disappointed to learn that these are just a few samples from an almost endless array of possibilities. These and other stems provided throughout this book are the synthesis of question types from numerous sites identified on page 198 in Chapter 7. Moreover, the intent here is not test prep, but understanding the rigor for its impact on instruction. For that purpose, there is much we can learn from these items.

We can see which standards receive the greatest emphasis for the teaching of skills (as opposed to reasoning and synthesis of knowledge, Depths of Knowledge 3 and 4). With a little more digging, we can also determine the format that these DOK items will take, the challenges of the academic language contained in the items, the broader reach of some of these standards—and the instructional implications of all of the above.

Standards Emphasized for DOK 2

Although it is true that all standards are important at all grade levels, it is also true that some standards are more closely aligned with Depths of Knowledge 1 and 2, whereas others generally tap deeper thinking, as expressed in Depths of Knowledge 3 and 4. Even a quick perusal of the question stems in Figure 2.2 demonstrates this. Beyond Standard 1, the standards most often matched to Depth of Knowledge 2 (application of skills and concepts) are Standards 2, 3, 4, and 5. This is because these standards are tied to the basic content and craft of a text, understanding that can be determined from the text without much interpretation. The response is right or it is wrong, and we can point to evidence in the text that justifies our answer. It is also true that the expectations for these standards can be amped up to challenge students at deeper Depths of Knowledge, which we will explore more fully in later chapters.

Although assessing standards at Depth of Knowledge 2 may appear to be familiar territory, we will miss our mark if we don't acknowledge that only *some* of this territory is familiar. Open the teacher's guide to any literacy program and you will find questions galore about the *content* of a text—themes and main ideas, characters, and plot development, the focus of Standards 2 and 3. But how many questions do you see, like those in Figure 2.2, related to craft and structure (Standards 4–6) and the integration of knowledge and ideas (Standards 7–9)?

Regarding craft and structure, we can't become complacent about Standard 4 (vocabulary) even at the DOK 2 level, because of the many concepts involved (synonyms, figurative language, and multiple-meaning words, to name a few) and the heavy emphasis on determining meaning from context. Standard 5 (text structure and genre) is largely uncharted territory, and without an awareness of the basics involved here for Depth of Knowledge 2, students will be unprepared to cope with its increased rigor at DOK 3. Standard 6 (purpose and point of view) always requires inferential thinking, and hence is not typically a DOK 2 expectation.

Although the integration of knowledge and ideas (Standards 7–9) would seem to address thinking beyond straightforward answers, a basic understanding of the role of illustrations (a component of Standard 7) is sometimes examined, especially in the primary grades. Standard 8 (use of evidence and

FIGURE 2.2 | Sample Assessment Items for DOK 2

Reading Standard 1: Textual evidence
· Which [two] details support the <u>conclusion</u>: _____?

Reading Standard 2: Development of central ideas
· What is the meaning of the quote ["_____"]? Explain it in your own words.   · Which sentence in the passage best describes the lesson?   · Choose a sentence that best summarizes the central idea [or main idea].   · Which statements belong in a summary of [this story], and which statements should be left out?   · What is the <u>best</u> summary of [paragraphs 4 and 5]?   · Which <u>two</u> claims does the author develop in this article?   · Which sentence states the theme of this part of the text?   · What is the author's main focus in this passage?

Reading Standard 3: Story/text components and relationship among story parts or parts of an informational text
· Which words below best describe [character A]?   · Which word describes how _____ was feeling?   · Where does the setting change?   · What is the main problem in the story?   · Arrange the events from the passage in order.   · How are these events related to each other?   · Which event initiates the [rising action] of the excerpt?

Reading Standard 4: Vocabulary in context
· What is the meaning of [<u>calamity</u>] in paragraph 7?   · Part A: What is the meaning of <u>calamity</u> in paragraph 7?   · Part B: Which of the following in the article might represent a [<u>calamity</u>] to the author?   · Choose the word in the paragraph that most closely resembles the definition provided.   · What does the word [<u>pen</u>] mean as it is used in paragraph 5?   · What is the meaning of [<u>raining cats and dogs</u>] as it is used in paragraph 3?   · What does the author tell the reader by using the underlined phrase?   · The Latin root *spectare* means "to watch." Which phrase best states the meaning of *spectacular*?   · What does the prefix [*in-*] mean in the word _____?   · Which of these is a synonym of the underlined word?   · The student wants to make sure that his words convince his audience to _____. Choose **two** words that would best replace the underlined word.

Reading Standard 5: Text features, structure, and genre
· Which text feature tells about the [photo]?   · What information can you get from this [graph]?   · What is the overall structure of most paragraphs in the article?   · What kind of information is the author giving us in this part of the [article]?

FIGURE 2.2 | (*continued*)

Reading Standard 5: Text features, structure, and genre—(*continued*)

· What craft is the author using in this part of the text?
· How is [paragraph A] connected to [paragraph B]?
· How is [paragraph 3] different from [paragraph 2]?
· Which part of the article helps the reader understand _____?
· How can the reader tell this is a [free-verse poem]?
· What is the most likely reason the author included _____ in the passage?

Reading Standard 7: Illustrations and other nonprint sources

· What part of the [story] does this [illustration] show?
· Which idea from the article is supported by the [photograph]?

Standard 8: Use of evidence and reasoning

· What kind of evidence does the author provide to support the point that _____?
· What reason does the author provide to support the point that _____?
· How does the author support the claim that _____? (grade 6)

Writing: Revising and editing for organization, elaboration, and clarity

· Reorder the sentences in this paragraph so the best beginning comes first.
· Where in the report should the student place information about _____ from [source 1]?
· Which source would most likely contain information about _____?
· In which source would you find information about _____?
· Choose [two sentences] that would add the best support _____.
· Choose the best beginning sentence to introduce this story.
· Which statement would be the best [ending] for this [letter]?
· Select the best sentence to transition between paragraphs.
· Choose a word to make your meaning clearer.

reasoning) has its roots at the DOK 2 level, again essential to students' agility in handling the more likely demands of this standard at Depth of Knowledge 3. Standard 9 (synthesizing information) requires text connections, beyond the scope of skill application.

Like the Reading items, DOK 2 Writing items examine students' understanding of key components of writing, not their own writing competence. Do students recognize good organization when they see it? Are they aware of which sources would be the most useful to researching a topic? What makes a good beginning or ending of a piece of writing? Which detail or word should be added for elaboration or clarity? Let's examine a few of these items more closely to better understand the instructional implications.

The Format of DOK 2 Items

One of the realities of Depth of Knowledge 2 that is not immediately obvious from the question stems is that most of these appear on the new assessments as selected-response (multiple-choice) items. As discussed in Chapter 1, this doesn't mean our goal is to supply students with abundant multiple-choice questions when measuring their DOK 2 performance. However, this format does signal something we should consider when teaching reading or any discipline: it's easier to *recognize* a correct response than it is to *retrieve* a piece of knowledge from memory and then *produce* a response yourself (Budiu, 2014).

Academic Language and Visual Support for DOK 2

Beyond an understanding of the words for basic literary concepts noted in Chapter 1, what additional language complexities might make it difficult for students to achieve the rigor of DOK 2? One obstacle will be the language of the questions.

Questions can be confusing for various reasons. But one obstacle that makes answering difficult is that different terminology may be used for concepts that are essentially the same. This point applies equally to the language used for questions within all Depths of Knowledge. The most obvious example of this is the language used in Standard 2 to specify a text's central idea. Here are some examples:

- Which sentence best describes the *lesson* that Rabbit learns?
- Which sentence best describes the *main idea* in paragraph 3?
- Which sentence best summarizes the *central idea* of the text?
- What is the *theme* of this poem?

There are other labels used as well. Perceptive teachers note the nuances of this terminology. A *lesson* isn't exactly a *main idea*, isn't exactly a *theme*. We stress over subtle differences between a central idea and an author's message—or any of the other labels we see here. Big hint: stop stressing, because this language on new assessments is all asking for the same thing.

We need to teach the *concept* (central idea, or whichever label you prefer). But beyond that, what we really need to teach is versatility in toggling between terms. Here's a perfect opportunity for another anchor chart. List the terms that mean the same as, or are close to, *theme* and offer this simple advice: "When the question asks you for the *central idea* or any other word you see here, it's the same as *theme, main idea,* or *lesson.* You already know what those terms mean."

Then, to give students practice recognizing a theme, a DOK 2 task, consider moving beyond an anchor chart of theme words to a Theme Comparison Chart. Figure 2.3 shows an example of such a chart based on picture books students might read in the intermediate grades.

Anchor and comparison charts are ever-evolving. The one in Figure 2.3 is mostly filled in. But it would begin as a blank form with only a few themes

noted. As the class completes a book for close reading, students decide which
of the themes apply to their text and write the title or affix a cover image in
the appropriate cell. *Recognizing* the theme is the extent of DOK 2 rigor. But a
couple of additional benefits of such charts are that students inevitably discover
a text where the theme is not already represented on the chart: "I don't think the
theme of this book is on our chart," a 3rd grader observed as her class contem-
plated the author's message in *A Bad Case of Stripes*, by David Shannon. "This
story is about being true to yourself, no matter what anyone else thinks." As this
incident illustrates, students begin to move beyond *recognizing* a theme to *producing* one—a DOK 3 task. When books with similar themes are identified side
by side, there's also potential for comparing texts based on theme (or whatever
the defining characteristic might be)—a challenge for DOK 4 later on.

FIGURE 2.3 | Theme Comparison Chart

Themes	Book 1	Book 2	Book 3	Book 4
Never give up on your dreams	*The Boy Who Harnessed the Wind,* by William Kamkwamba	*Sonia Sotomayor,* by Jonah Winter	*More Than Anything Else,* by Marie Bradby	*Snowflake Bentley,* by Jacqueline Briggs Martin
Stand up for what is important to you	*Brave Girl: Clara and the Shirtwaist Makers' Strike of 1909,* by Michelle Markel	*The Summer My Father Was Ten,* by Pat Brisson	*The Librarian of Basra: A True Story from Iraq,* by Jeanette Winter	*Up the Learning Tree,* by Marcia Vaughan
Accept others' differences	*Sister Anne's Hands,* by Mary-beth Lorbiecki	*One Green Apple,* by Eve Bunting	*Eggbert: The Slightly Cracked Egg,* by Tom Ross	*Be Good to Eddie Lee,* by Virginia Fleming
The pain of racial injustice	*The Other Side,* by Jacqueline Woodson	*White Socks Only,* by Evelyn Coleman	*Freedom Summer,* by Deborah Wiles	*Freedom School, Yes!* by Amy Littlesugar
Honesty is the best policy	*The Honest to Goodness Truth,* by Patricia McKissack	*The Empty Pot,* by Demi	*The Wolf Who Cried Boy,* by Bob Hartman	*A Day's Work,* by Eve Bunting

To get you started, find a blank Theme Comparison Chart (Figure 7.20) on page 183 in Chapter 7. In the same chapter, you'll also find an anchor chart, Words That Mean About the Same as *Theme* (Figure 7.14), on page 177.

Where to Increase Instructional Focus for DOK 2

Beyond supporting students with anchor and comparison charts, we need to recognize instructional practices that are important to successful application of skills and concepts. Some of the DOK 2 question stems alert us to areas that may need more attention. Let's look closely, standard by standard.

Standard 2

- *Explain it in your own words.*

Are we spending enough time teaching students to paraphrase? This is an effective way to check for comprehension and is especially useful with English learners and students with low language skills. For paraphrasing, we are working with short portions of a text, not a whole story or article.

- *Which statements belong in a summary of [this story], and which statements should be left out?*

As with all DOK 2 tasks, the challenge here is not to *produce* a summary but to understand what a summary *is*. Summarizing is a critical skill. Are we giving students enough strategies to recognize a good summary when they see one, or to know which sentences belong in a summary and which ones should be eliminated? We could teach them the strategy *Somebody wanted _____, but _____, so _____*, which works some of the time. We could teach them that only *actions*, not *descriptions*, belong in a summary. We could teach them other techniques as well. The point is, they need multiple ways to approach summarizing because texts are different and don't all call for the same summarizing technique.

Standard 3

- *Which event [initiates the rising action] of the story?*

Assessment items contain many references to plot structure. Are we doing enough with the tried-and-true plot pyramid we may remember from our own school days? These are easy to access online, with varying levels of complexity to fit whatever grade you teach.

Standard 4

- *The Latin root* spectare *means "to watch." Which phrase best states the meaning of* spectacular?

There may be other components of vocabulary you could add to your classroom to-do list, but many teachers concur that more attention to Greek and Latin roots is in order. How do you make sure that your students receive systematic instruction in roots, prefixes, and suffixes? How do you plan for a continuum of instruction in this area across grade levels?

Standard 5

- *What is the overall structure of most paragraphs in the article?*
- *What kind of information is the author giving us in this part of the [article]?*
- *What craft is the author using in this part of the text?*
- *How is [paragraph A] connected to [paragraph B]?*
- *How is [paragraph 3] different from [paragraph 2]?*
- *Which part of the article helps the reader understand _____?*
- *How can the reader tell this is a [free verse poem]?*

With the possible exclusion of informational text features, virtually every aspect of Standard 5 needs more attention in most classrooms. This is our most glaring literacy need, the "big black hole" of the reading curriculum. In our defense, text structure as it is viewed today is a new expectation—or at the very least, an expectation that has transformed significantly since bygone decades. Back then, the goal was knowledge of a few rudimentary external structures like cause/effect, compare/contrast, main idea/details, and sequence of events. Now our students need to be familiar with a greater range of external structures and genres, and the much more challenging complexities of *internal* crafting.

The biggest challenge of Standard 5, I believe, is that we look at question stems such as those in the list and we still have no idea of what we need to teach so students understand the role of structure in the crafting of a text. However, if we look at the response options, we begin to peel away some of this uncertainty.

Look at the sample items in Figures 2.4 and 2.5 and the response options that tap comprehension of external structures. We see from some of the options in Figure 2.4—"randomly," "argumentatively"—that there are more structures

FIGURE 2.4 | Grade 6 Sample Item

Part A: In what way does the text present information?

A. randomly

B. sequentially

C. argumentatively

D. comparatively

Source: From *Grade 6: Countdown to Common Core Assessments: English Language Arts* (p. 12), by McGraw-Hill Education, © 2015, New York: McGraw-Hill Education.

to which students should be introduced than we may have considered previously. Moreover, we see from the item in Figure 2.5 that understanding external structure is not merely a function of memorizing a handful of defined formats, but also demonstrating a more thorough understanding of an author's organizational strategy. These concepts are teachable, but we need to take the time to ask these questions and help students examine the craft of a text in addition to its content.

FIGURE 2.5 | Grade 5 Sample Item

Part A: Which sentence describes how the story is organized?

A. It is divided into two parts based on the time of year.

B. It is divided into two parts based on Desiree and her mom's point of view.

C. It is divided into three parts based on the different schools that Desiree attends.

D. It is divided into three parts based on the different experiences Desiree has at school.

Source: From *Grade 5: Countdown to Common Core Assessments: English Language Arts* (p. 5), by McGraw-Hill Education, © 2015, New York: McGraw-Hill Education.

The same is true for building an appreciation of a text's internal structure. Figure 2.6 shows a grade 3 example. Before we can help our students understand the function of different parts of a passage, we need to train ourselves to examine a text in this way. This is a first step in reading like a writer. If students can recognize how an author is putting ideas together, maybe their own writing will begin to reflect better organization.

FIGURE 2.6 | Grade 3 Sample Item

What is the most likely reason the author included the legend in the passage? Pick two choices.

☐ to make the idea of tasting sap seem fun

☐ to provide details about the Iroquois way of life

☐ to explain how people discovered how to make syrup

☐ to show sap has been used to make syrup for many years

☐ to provide information that shows that sap is a good sweetener for food

☐ to show how the Iroquois used to make syrup and how syrup is made today

Source: From *Smarter Balanced Assessment Consortium ELA Practice Test Scoring Guide Grade 3* (p. 22). ©2017 The Regents of California. https://portal.smarterbalanced.org/library/en/grade-3-ela-practice-test-scoring-guide.pdf

And the same is true of authors' crafts. DOK 2 questions like those in Figure 2.7 might be present at any grade level, and although right now students may regard them as challenging, such questions really address very basic understanding: naming a craft and explaining its meaning. Students will feel more confident with authors' crafts if we regularly note them in texts we read and follow up with an expectation for students to include crafts in *their* writing. To get you started, two templates for the most common crafts present in both literary and informational texts are provided on pages 169–170 in Chapter 7 (Figures 7.8 and 7.9).

FIGURE 2.7 | Author's Crafts Sample Item

Part A: The underlined phrase in this passage is an example of which figure of speech?

A. personification

B. a metaphor

C. a simile

D. an idiom

Part B: What does this figure of speech show?

A. The size of a red-eyed tree frog

B. The color of the frog's eyes

C. The frog's shocking appearance

D. The frog's appetite

Standard 7

• *What part of the [story] does this [illustration] show?*

There is nothing noteworthy about this question itself. However, it is an apt reminder that examining illustrations is useful *after* reading as a comprehension check. When we spend time *before* reading doing a picture walk or analyzing graphics, we are reducing students' need to get meaning by reading closely. We are also opening the door to predictions that may be misleading. But *after* reading, students should be able to articulate the role of the image in supporting the text.

Standard 8

• *What kind of evidence does the author provide to support the point that _____?*

This is the other standard, in addition to Standard 5, that most confuses teachers. What does it mean when the question asks, "What kind of evidence does the author provide to support this point?" Again, it's hard to understand exactly what this is asking without seeing some response options. For clarification, see the grade 4 sample in Figure 2.8.

FIGURE 2.8 | Grade 4 Sample Item

Part A: What type of evidence does the author provide to support the point that the sand at Fort Myers Beach is "perfect" for sculpting?

A. interviews with judges of the competition

B. statistics about the size of the sand grains

C. opinions from professional sand sculptors

D. experiences of visitors to the competition

Source: From *Grade 4: Countdown to Common Core Assessments: English Language Arts* (p. 10), by McGraw-Hill Education, © 2015, New York: McGraw-Hill Education.

Standard 8 also addresses the *quality* of evidence, so much of this standard will require interpretation, better suited to Depths of Knowledge 3 and 4. But when we're just identifying the *kind* of evidence, that's DOK 2. The challenge is that students need to know what types of information "count" as evidence. In this case, it could be interviews, statistics, opinions, or experiences, though we could add to that list with sources like facts, personal examples, speeches, and quotations.

The message to us as teachers is that we should be using all these sources of information (and evidence) in our literacy instruction. When would it be useful for students to read interviews or listen to speeches? Where would statistics or facts strengthen students' knowledge of a topic? Understanding how to use different kinds of evidence will provide students the foundation they need for deeper thinking.

Writing standards

The writing applications for DOK 2 should not pose problems to students if they understand basic elements of authors' craft like organization and elaboration and if they are experienced with the writing process, especially revising and editing. However, these may be big "ifs"—addressed through the writing curriculum, more than the reading curriculum. We can begin by thinking about the kinds of complex texts we might use to connect reading and writing.

> **Bottom Line for Aligning Rigor and Standards for DOK 2:** The rigor for standards at this Depth of Knowledge resides in an understanding of the *concepts* upon which skills are built. For example, before students can identify a good summary, they need to know what a good summary *is*. Before they can name the correct figure of speech, they must be able to define *metaphor, simile, idiom*, and *personification*.

Aligning Rigor and Text Complexity for DOK 2

Appendix A of the Common Core State Standards gave us four qualitative complexities for choosing text, all of which work very well for Depth of Knowledge 2: knowledge demands, language, structure, and meaning. Each of these qualities has implications for rigor.

Knowledge Demands

Think of knowledge demands as prior knowledge, the background students bring to a text that makes the subject accessible. For example, stories or articles that take place in unfamiliar geographical regions or within diverse cultures can be difficult for some students with a limited worldview. Sources like these can be a stretch for readers if they lack sufficient knowledge in an area. But here's something to think about: if we want reading to challenge students, we don't want to dismiss these texts too quickly, even for skill-building lessons. When a reader can't fall back on what he already knows about a subject to construct meaning and must rely completely on the text for comprehension, it's imperative to read carefully to get meaning.

Language

Laura Robb, an educator I respect a lot, titled a recent book *Vocabulary Is Comprehension* (Robb, 2014). In so many ways, that notion is spot-on, especially for informational text. If students understand the key words and how they fit together, they probably have a grasp of the basic content. Providing opportunities for rigor for DOK 2 means we need to choose books with words that students can add to their vocabulary so they can articulate their understanding of a topic with greater precision. What words do students need to know to talk about the main idea of a nonfiction article about the solar system or the character traits of Paul Bunyan? They will need to understand and recognize these words in skill-based assessment items.

Structure

A third area of qualitative complexity is the structure of the text. If students enter the primary grades with any understanding of writing structures, it's the traditional problem/solution format that they know: "Once upon a time" to "happily ever after." But this barely scratches the surface of the structural knowledge students will need, even for Depth of Knowledge 2. As noted in the assessment items, there are abundant text structures and features with which students will need to be familiar, as well as internal aspects of structure. Think outside the box for this. For literary text, consider classic poetry, excerpts from classic children's literature, and traditional tales. For information, consider primary sources like a diary or journal entry, an essay, a speech, or a letter.

Meaning

In any conversation about literacy, meaning always plays an important role. Complex meaning is closely connected to the degree of abstract or inferential thinking involved. It might be evident in more complicated themes or multiple themes, or in robust characters and multifaceted problems. We want complex meaning within the texts we choose for DOK 2 because these same sources will be a springboard for students' thinking at DOK 3.

Texts that support meaning and other complexities for DOK 2 will align easily to the components of literacy featured in Reading Standards 2–5: strong central ideas, intricate development of ideas, opportunities for determining word meanings from context, and interesting structural elements. Sources should also be well written, so students can witness craft in action. *All* texts include evidence, Standard 1, and a focus on Standards 6–9 is better suited to Depths of Knowledge 3 and 4. The exemplary sources below come from the Bibliography of Student Resources at the end of this book. They will all work well for specific skill focus.

Texts for grades K–2 students

- *Eggbert*, **by Tom Ross**, a sweet allegory about a little egg who doesn't fit in, is perfect for examining central ideas.
- **"The Wind," by James Reeves**, a short poem with some archaic language, works well for defining words through context.
- *Turtle, Turtle, Watch Out!* by April Pulley Sayre, is an informational narrative that makes facts about saving sea turtles interesting through its story format. It's great for focusing on craft, with its repeated pattern and circular ending.
- *Never Smile at a Monkey*, **by Steve Jenkins**, shows the development of main ideas, with strange-but-true facts about different animals and ample supporting details.

- *Wonders of the World* (ReadWorks) presents information about six famous landmarks with a clear organizational structure that supports young readers.

Texts for grades 3–5 students

- *Martin's Big Words: The Life of Dr. Martin Luther King, Jr.*, by Doreen Rappaport, has it all: an important message, interesting structure, and plenty of craft. But the element that stands out most of all is the language. Understanding the rich vocabulary in this book, some of which is embedded in quotes, is a necessary first step in unlocking meaning.
- "Mother to Son," by Langston Hughes, is a poem superbly crafted in its use of extended metaphor: climbing a set of rickety stairs as a metaphor for surviving life's struggles.
- *Mercedes and the Chocolate Pilot: A True Story of the Berlin Airlift and the Candy That Dropped from the Sky*, by Margot Theis Raven, is a touching, true story about the Berlin Airlift that offers intermediate-grade students multiple themes to ponder. It also relies on the Epilogue for delivering its message, an interesting use of structure.
- *Voices in the Park*, by Anthony Browne, is a good example of a unique text structure. Four voices tell their own version of a story about the same afternoon in the park.
- *The Summer My Father Was Ten*, by Pat Brisson, includes everything we look for in a well-crafted narrative: well-developed characters, an interesting problem, and a satisfying resolution.

Texts for grades 6–8 students

- "Letter from Jackie Robinson on Civil Rights" (ReadWorks) uses language that is both formal and archaic to send a strong message to President Eisenhower about the decades-long plight of African Americans.
- *The Wretched Stone*, by Chris Van Allsburg, is a fantasy told as a series of journal entries. This structure adds intrigue as readers piece together the clues to solve this mystery of the identity of the wretched stone.
- *Fox*, by Margaret Wild, is ideal for examining craft. How does the way print is displayed on a page contribute to the author's message?
- *Encounter*, by Jane Yolen, is the story of the arrival of Columbus from a Taino Indian boy's perspective—a vivid example of how point of view affects the way a story is told.
- *Taking Down the Green-Eyed Monster*, by Margie Markarian (Weekly Reader/ReadWorks) works well for examining the development of ideas because of its use of headings and subheadings.

> **Bottom Line for Aligning Rigor and Text Complexity for DOK 2:**
> Although all books and other resources provide opportunities
> for tapping multiple complexities, some sources feature complex
> language with rather straightforward meaning, whereas others
> may use very simple language to convey complex ideas. Recog-
> nizing the specific complexities of different resources will help
> you choose texts that cover the full spectrum of complexities
> matched to different standards.

Aligning Rigor and Close Reading for DOK 2

We get a mixed message about the need to teach comprehension skills in the
context of close reading. Few close reading references mention skill instruction.
The general view is that if students read a text closely and understand it deeply,
they will be able to respond to all kinds of questions—without spending time
on individual skills. However, David Coleman and Susan Pimentel (2012), two
lead authors of the Common Core, say this in their "Revised Publishers' Criteria"
document:

> Students need to build an infrastructure of skills, habits, knowledge,
> dispositions, and experience that enables them to approach new challeng-
> ing texts with confidence and stamina. As much as possible, this training
> should be embedded in the activity of reading the text rather than being
> taught as a separate body of material.

My work in classrooms validates both views. We can certainly reduce the
need for skills instruction with the deeper textual analysis of close reading. But
what if students don't even understand the concept behind a skill, like the meaning of "theme" or "turning point"? What if they've never been exposed to "authors'
crafts" and have no idea what evidence they're looking for in the crafting of a
text? We may be taking a big chance if we don't address these skill needs head-on.
Hence, the big question is not whether to teach comprehension skills, but where
we should position this instruction within our literacy curriculum. Moreover,
what defines high-quality skills teaching that leads to student rigor?

Unlike comprehension instruction of the past, in which teaching reading
meant leading students through a series of skills lessons, our current emphasis
on close reading suggests that we teach an appreciation of the text as a whole
during an initial read. This is reading as *art*. We can invite students to apply
strategies for independent close reading suggested in Chapter 1. Doing so will
prepare them for the rigor of Depths of Knowledge 1 and 2. We can add text-
dependent questions too, to check for understanding.

But if students' responses from an initial close reading reveal a weak grasp of something important to the text—perhaps confusion about the main idea, the external structure, or something else—we need to address this. Perhaps the deficit resulted from carelessness in the first round of reading. Correcting it may be a simple matter of rereading. We can use graphic organizers like Finding Evidence as I Read Literature, or Finding Evidence as I Read Information (Figures 7.5 and 7.6, respectively, pages 166–167 in Chapter 7) to keep students focused. However, no amount of "read it again" will fix a weakness if the problem is lack of conceptual understanding. For this we need skill instruction.

Close Reading Shifts for DOK 2

For students to be successful at Depth of Knowledge 2, we need to hunker down and teach the *concept*, whatever it may be, so students become skilled in the rigor that DOK 2 requires. Teaching skills of reading comprehension is the instructional essence of Depth of Knowledge 2. Many skills may warrant reinforcement, beginning with the areas of need designated by the sample items cited earlier. Skills instruction could occur as a follow-up to an initial close reading lesson with the whole class. But it will be most effective in small groups, with text at students' instructional level. Now we need to consider what it means to teach these skills *well*.

Teaching Comprehension Skills Well

How will we know when we have taught a comprehension skill *well*? Let's return to the definition of rigor for Depth of Knowledge 2: *independence in applying literacy skills and concepts accurately*. We are well acquainted with the criteria for *accuracy*, for what good is a skill that is inaccurate? But applying a skill *independently* is a principle that previously we may not have considered strongly enough—and we should.

Unless students can use a skill on their own, without teacher guidance, what are the chances they'll be able to apply it when they need it most—on an assessment or to solve a problem beyond the classroom? Teaching skills to the threshold of independence is a function of the *science* of reading, step by step. We refer to this as explicit instruction or the gradual release of responsibility.

Gradual Release of Responsibility

Gradual release of responsibility is not a new idea. This instructional model harkens back to the 1980s and the work of Pearson and Gallagher (1983). The idea is that at the beginning of the instructional process, the teacher controls the learning, heavily supporting students. This typically includes explaining the new skill or concept to be learned and modeling it. Gradually, the teacher transitions to prompting students to respond to questions related to the new learning. Then students practice with a partner or on their own. If all goes well, by the end of the lesson (or after a few lessons), the teacher has relinquished all responsibility to students and is no longer needed for support. Students perform the skill both accurately and independently. This explicit model makes wonderful sense, but we have not been wonderfully successful in putting it into practice.

Let's look at the steps in the gradual release process, what each step entails, and how we will know when our explicit instruction has gone off track. Here are the steps I propose, slightly modified from Pearson's original model:

- Link
- Explain
- Model
- Pause and prompt
- Guided practice (with feedback)
- Independence
- Reflection

Link to the past and the future

Make sure students see the connection between today's skill lesson and a lesson that preceded it: "Remember yesterday when we worked on text structure and learned how to figure out whether the text was problem/solution or sequence of events? Today we're going to look at another way an author might organize an article. In today's lesson, I'll show you how to do this. Then I'll give you a couple of articles and ask you to find examples of the structure yourself."

Although the connection to past learning might seem obvious to you, students are not so quick to determine this for themselves. They will approach the lesson more confidently if they recognize that it builds on something they already know. Likewise, they'll be more purposeful learners if they are aware upfront that their future holds some accountability to the lesson content.

Some lessons are doomed before they begin because the teacher jumps right in without setting the stage. And there is no mention of student expectations after the lesson. Don't skip this part. I'm always amazed at how surprised students are when I let them know there will be a follow-up task for them to demonstrate their learning—like this is quite a novel idea. Still, they sit a little straighter and engage more fully after getting this heads-up.

Explain the skill

As teachers, we think we're great explainers. After all, we do this all day long in one form or another. But explaining a skill is different and, oddly, where our explicit instruction is most likely to go off track. "Today we're going to work on compare/contrast text structure." This is a reasonable place to begin, naming the skill. But it fails to guide students forward. Explanations should guide—clarify not just *what* the skill is, but *how* to achieve success with it. What students need to know most is the kind of evidence to look for to justify their thinking.

Let's suppose we're teaching the compare/contrast text structure, using an article (which needs to focus on pairs of ideas—like alligators and crocodiles, or a democracy and a monarchy). What do students need to understand to apply this skill competently? There's no list of absolutes, but we might share these hints with students:

- To *compare*, look for signal words that show similarity—such as *both, alike, same, too, also, as well as, similar, in common*.
- To *contrast*, look for signal words that show differences—such as *although, however, but, yet, differ, unlike, on the contrary, while, unless, on the other hand, even though, instead*.
- Look for the details that follow these signal words. Make sure you can find at least one similarity and one difference (two would be better).
- You might want to organize your information into a T-chart to show the similarities and differences between your ideas.

I call a list of hints like this a "target," and I provided 50 of them on a CD in my book *That's a Great Answer: Teaching Literature Response Strategies to Elementary, ELL, and Struggling Readers* (2012). Aim for the bull's-eye! The steps are identified in a short list on a chart along with an image of a target. I explain the skill, one step at a time before reading, and return to points as needed as the lesson progresses. What we're really doing here is breaking down our own thinking process so students see there is a *strategy* for approaching the skill. It's easy, and it works. Any strategy you can suggest for approaching a skill is helpful.

Model

Although we may be guilty of too little careful explaining in the past, we've probably engaged in too much modeling. I know this statement contradicts current rhetoric, but it's true. Although the intent of demonstrating strategic thinking to students was well meaning, we've sometimes gotten lost in "model lesson land," with too much teacher-talk and not enough student interaction. This modeling typically went on for interminable minutes, while students began rolling around on the floor or showing us in other ways that they had tuned us out. Modeling was also regarded as a distinct lesson component, following an explanation of the skill and preceding what followed.

Modeling a single example should be enough. An explicit lesson, while intentionally thorough, should be short—no more than 15 or 20 minutes. Most of this time should be spent with *students* doing the work, not you. Find one place in the text to show how the skill is applied, and don't be afraid to involve students in small ways: "Right here, I'm noticing that there are two ideas discussed in this article, so maybe the author is comparing and contrasting. I can see that one idea is *alligators*. Who can find the other idea and underline it on our whiteboard?" Now move on to prompt students. You can model again at any point in a lesson to clear up confusion.

Pause and prompt

Pausing to prompt marks the beginning of the gradual release. For example, consider this statement from an article about the difference between alligators and crocodiles: "Snout shape: Alligators have wider, U-shaped snouts, while crocodile front ends are more pointed and V-shaped" (Bryner, 2012). You might begin by asking, "Do we have a clue here about whether the author is giving us a similarity or a difference? What's the signal word?" Return to the target criteria if necessary so students can identify the word *while*, which signifies a contrast.

You can gradually move to even less guidance by pausing without a specific prompt: "Why do you think I stopped at the end of this paragraph? Do we have any new evidence?" The amount of time you spend pausing and prompting will depend on the quality of your students' responses. When they seem to be catching on, step back by giving them more to do on their own.

Guided practice

This might be a good time for partner work, or students can work by themselves, if you prefer: "Read the next paragraph with your reading buddy. Find at least one piece of evidence including a signal word. Decide whether the author is comparing or contrasting." One important consideration when choosing any text for skill instruction is to make sure there are ample opportunities within the reading for both modeling and practicing.

Independence

You may not get to complete independence after every explicit lesson, as some students may need more guided practice. But students should be able to show you what they know with an accountable task. In this case, they might finish reading the article at their seat and find additional evidence. Or, for more rigor, they could read a new article and enter their evidence onto a T-chart showing similarities and differences. Ultimately, the expectation could be to read a new article and produce a constructed response to a compare/contrast question.

Reflection

Regardless of the level of independence, a good skill lesson should conclude with a few moments for students to reflect on their learning. Resist the temptation to sum up the lesson yourself, as the goal is to discover whether students are aware of their own thinking process. "If someone was absent from our class today, how could we explain to them what we learned about comparing and contrasting?" I like this question because if students can articulate the steps in applying a skill, there's a better chance they'll be able to transfer that thinking to another task that requires the same steps.

I also like to ask students what they think we should do tomorrow based on our progress today. Doing so establishes the link we need to the next lesson and encourages self-regulation: *Do I need more practice with what we worked on today, or am I ready to move on?* Moving on might mean adding more rigor to expectations—for example, asking students to distinguish between the three organizational structures they have now learned. Or it might mean setting the criteria for an independent written response appropriate to Depth of Knowledge 2.

For teacher reflection, my favorite question is this: *What can my students do more independently today than they could do yesterday?* If we can measure even some small growth day by day, eventually we will reach the Big Goal: students applying skills in writing, on their own, no teacher scaffolding needed. To pursue independent written response, let's first consider how best to align rigor and student interaction.

Bottom Line for Aligning Rigor and Close Reading for DOK 2: Success for students at Depth of Knowledge 2 is contingent on strong literacy skills, and strong literacy skills are based on *independent* skill application. Nothing will be more important to students' independent use of skills than vigilance in the gradual release of responsibility, from heavy teacher scaffolding to no scaffolding at all.

Aligning Rigor and Student Interaction for DOK 2

Like Depth of Knowledge 1, oral response for DOK 2 will not center on deep conversation. Again, at this level, with answers that are either right or wrong, there will not be much verbal exchange once a correct response has been shared. Still, oral response is important, especially as it ultimately supports written response, and interaction will be instrumental in helping students reach this goal. Think: oral rehearsal.

Oral Rehearsal

Although the concept of oral rehearsal is a familiar one and the term has been around for a while, there is no uniformly accepted definition. For our purpose in determining its relevance to Depth of Knowledge, let's regard oral rehearsal as oral response that precedes written response.

There are two points to consider. First, if students can't "say it," it's doubtful they'll be able to "write it." Second, even if students can talk about something knowledgeably, a worthy written response is more than "talk written down." Providing opportunities to talk about a response is a good place to begin for the rigor of Depth of Knowledge 2. But *how* to translate spoken language into written language is a necessary next step.

Collaborative Talk

Talking with a partner or a small group about an answer to a question helps students in several ways. Students solidify their own thinking as they listen to the thinking of their peers. They consider the organization of their response and which details work best for elaboration. Disconnected words and phrases roaming free in their minds become logically constructed sentences as they strive to make their response meaningful to those who listen. Along the way, they gain confidence: *My response sounded good. No one laughed. I'm ready to put my answer on paper.*

Sometimes just giving students the chance to say their response out loud is enough. But we also know we have students who get their oral message across adequately and still struggle with getting the same answer down on paper. Why is this? There are differences between speech and writing.

Differences Between Speech and Writing

Writing uses more varied vocabulary than speaking. In writing, phrases and clauses are often longer, with more formal syntax and grammar. An answer may need quotation marks and commas and apostrophes in the right places to ensure that it makes sense.

Speaking provides a context. It offers a stronger sense of audience, and a speaker can watch the body language of audience members (a group of kids, for example) to know when someone is confused or disapproves. Listeners can even interrupt to ask questions when the speaker hasn't given them enough information. In the end, a spoken response has to satisfy both the speaker and the audience. We can teach the skills of oral rehearsal to close the gap between speaking a response and writing one.

Teaching the Skills of Oral Rehearsal

The challenge here is to help students develop an oral response that is more like a written response than the informal voice they use when sharing ideas spontaneously with their peers.

Figure 2.9 presents some oral rehearsal criteria to get you started.

Once students have been introduced to these criteria, they will need to practice. Listen in as they respond out loud to a question with their partner. Begin with DOK 2 questions because these simply require textual information well stated, no in-depth interpretation.

Encourage students to monitor the quality of their responses using the Oral Rehearsal Checklist (Figure 7.2) on page 160 in Chapter 7. This checklist reminds students what should be included for an oral response that also meets the conditions of a strong written response. Add criteria for your grade level or academic disciplines as needed.

FIGURE 2.9 | How to Rehearse an Answer Orally Before Writing It

· Think about the people who will be reading your answer, and explain your ideas so they will understand what you mean.

· Answer the 5W/H questions if that information was in the text: *who, what, when, where, why, how.*

· Use words that connect parts of your answer, like *first, next, in conclusion.*

· Make sure events are in chronological order.

· Take out confusing pronouns and replace them with names and specific nouns (not *he, her, it,* but *Grandpa Bob, the babysitter, the collie*).

· Explain words that might be confusing to your audience.

· Think about what *else* your readers will want to know. What questions might they ask you if you read your answer to them?

> **Bottom Line for Aligning Rigor and Student Interaction for DOK 2:** Responding well to a question requires more than the right information—even when the question doesn't involve a lot of inferential thinking. A good answer is organized and moves from point to point clearly. Encourage students to *rehearse* their response before writing it for optimum DOK 2 performance.

Aligning Rigor and the Reading-Writing Connection for DOK 2

For Depth of Knowledge 2 on new assessments, students need only to recognize quality writing; they do not have to produce their own good writing. Items aligned to the Writing standards confirm this. But it's the Craft and Structure band of the Common Core *Reading* Standards that will help us address this need. Look back at the DOK 2 questions for Reading Standards 4 and 5 and you will see that the instructional challenge here is to help students read like writers.

Exactly what do we mean by "reading like a writer"? We mean that writing affects reading, and reading affects writing. The craft elements students identify in a text model the crafts they can incorporate into their own writing. Our job for the rigor of Depth of Knowledge 2 is to teach students what these craft elements are and how to recognize them when they see them.

The six writing traits—ideas, organization, word choice, fluency, voice, and presentation/contentions—made popular by Ruth Culham (2003) and others have become a means of bringing the reading-writing connection to life in the classroom. But sometimes I don't think these traits go far enough in helping teachers know just what they should teach for each trait. In Figure 2.10, I have identified specific crafts under every trait, along with a description of the craft. Once you know what you're looking for, it's easy to help your students find these crafts, too. You won't need an explicit lesson, but you *will* need texts that are well crafted so they can be used as mentor texts.

One simple way to provide practice locating these crafts is to use the templates provided in Chapter 7, on pages 169–170: Authors' Crafts in Literary Text (Figure 7.8) and Text Features and Authors' Crafts in Informational Text (Figure 7.9). Ask students to note where they found various craft elements in a text they are reading independently or for small-group instruction. Maybe they could find five crafts of their choice. Or you could identify for them the focus crafts. Depth of Knowledge 2 requires an awareness of the crafts that connect reading and writing. This will be an essential first step if students are to achieve the rigor of DOK 3, producing their own well-crafted writing, explained in the next chapter.

FIGURE 2.10 | Reading Like a Writer: Recognizing Authors' Crafts Related to Writing Traits

Developing an idea: Ideas make up the content of a piece of writing. For students to develop ideas well, we must help them recognize that good idea development is specific, not general.

Crafts to recognize for developing ideas:

· Writing "small"—small details that *show* rather than *tell*

· Snapshot—description of a person or a place

· Internal dialogue—thoughts that are in the character's head and shared with the reader but not shared with other characters

· Dialogue/conversation—places where the dialogue highlights the trait, motivation, or attitude of a character or a person

· Gestures—nodding, hands on hips, downcast eyes, or other small actions that show attitude

· A scene (or small moment) that includes snapshots, internal dialogue, dialogue, and gestures

Organization: Organization is the internal structure of a piece of writing, how the author puts it together. For students to organize a piece of writing well, they should begin with a clear purpose and proceed logically. Connections between ideas should be strong. The piece should close with a resolution, tying up loose ends and answering important questions.

Crafts that make a piece of writing fit together:

· Narrative—Organization that shows a unified plot; well-defined story parts, like characters and setting; clear transitions; logical sequence; and effective beginning and ending

· Opinion—Organization that shows purposeful focus throughout, an introduction that identifies position based on importance of the topic, logical progression of ideas, helpful transitions, opposing opinions (if required by standard at grade level), ending that shows implications of main points

· Informational—Organization that shows purposeful focus throughout, an introduction that states the main idea clearly, logical progression of ideas, useful transitions, ending that shows significance of main points

FIGURE 2.10 | (continued)

Word choice: Word choice is about the use of rich, colorful, precise language that communicates meaning not just in a functional way but also in a moving way. In good informational writing, word choice clarifies and expands ideas. In opinion writing, it moves readers to a new vision of things. In narrative writing, it creates images in readers' minds that are so real, they feel like they're a part of the story itself. Students need to notice the great words an author uses that create the mood or tone of a text.

Crafts that make words stand out:
· Words or phrases associated with a positive tone or a negative tone—e.g., "puffy white clouds floating gently across an azure sky"; "dark, angry thunderheads threatening doom from afar"
· Specific colors—e.g., *peach, aqua*
· Precise nouns—e.g., *collie* instead of *dog*; *tulip* instead of *flower*
· Great action words—e.g., *shimmer* instead of *shine*; *screech* instead of *yell*
· Exaggeration—hyperbole such as that found in tall tales
· Figurative language—similes, idioms, metaphors, personification
· Interesting character names—e.g., Pippi Longstocking, Kanga, and Roo; names that provide a sense of the character
· Made-up words—like those in Dr. Seuss books and elsewhere

Voice: Voice is what lets a reader know who is speaking and what is important to that person. In informational writing, it is the knowledge about the topic coming through loud and clear. In opinion or argument writing, it is the passion about the topic. In narrative writing, it is the way the author makes the story sound like it could really happen. (For example, if a child is talking, does the voice sound like a "real" kid?) Students need to look for the "personal flavor"— what makes *this* piece of writing sound like it could have been written by only *this* author.

Crafts that make a voice sound real:
· Informational writing—the author sounds like he knows a lot about the topic
· Opinion/argumentative writing—the author sounds like she really cares about the topic
· Narrative writing—the author/narrator expresses ideas the way a real person would express them
· Authors and characters that show *attitude*
· Writing from the point of view of something that doesn't talk (such as a truck or a tree)
· An unexpected point of view (like a story told from the wolf's point of view)
· Writing in dialect
· Writing that is written directly to "you" (second-person narrator)
· Writing in two or more voices

Fluency: Sentence fluency is what makes a piece of writing sound good when it is read out loud. The rhythm and flow of the words draw the reader in as much as the meaning of the words themselves. Sometimes the writer surprises the reader with short sentences or fragments. Sometimes long sentences are used to create images. Teach students to notice what makes the writing sound good when it is read aloud.

Crafts that add to the rhythm and flow of the language:
· Making a longer sentence from two short sentences
· Interesting sentence construction (sentences that begin with a phrase or clause, not a simple subject)
· Sentences that are different lengths, or show a pattern (like *short, short, long*)
· Alliteration (two or more words in a row that begin with the same sound)
· The same starting sound on multiple words in a sentence
· Repeated lines or phrases
· Transition sentences that connect one idea to another
· Sentence fragments

(continued)

FIGURE 2.10 | (continued)

Presentation and Conventions: Presentation relates to how the writing appears on the paper, how the writing looks. Conventions (e.g., punctuation and capitalization) make the text understandable in a uniform way. When it comes to craft, however, both conventions and presentation can be used creatively to draw the reader's eye to features the author wishes to highlight. Students should look for these features that make a piece of writing visually appealing or help parts of it stand out.

Crafts that make words and sentences stand out:

· Exclamation marks

· Bold letters

· Parentheses

· Shaping print in different ways

· Capital letters

· Italics

· Different font sizes

· Interesting arrangement of print

Bottom Line for Aligning Rigor and Reading-Writing Connections for DOK 2: The full weight of reading like a writer is evident at DOK 2. Students need to understand not only the writing traits but crafts that authors use within each trait. What is *hyperbole*? What is *dialect*? The more students are aware of different crafts and can recognize them as they read, the greater will be their foundation in this area for DOK 3 and DOK 4.

Aligning Rigor and Formative Assessment for DOK 2

Assessments aimed at measuring new standards such as the Common Core promote the notion that students are now tested more on the integration of knowledge than on specific skill applications. This is true for some items, especially performance-based tasks that require reading multiple passages. However, questions on portions of the assessment that measure literacy expertise after reading a single passage are almost always linked to one—and only one—standard (or skill) in addition to Standard 1, which focuses on the *evidence* to support a response.

Skill competence matters—which begs the question: How do we best assess skills in the classroom that measure the rigor of DOK 2 to inform our instruction? Establishing assessment priorities is important.

Earlier in this chapter, I provided an extensive list of questions for each standard that students would probably find on new standards-based assessments. Include them all in your instruction as they fit organically into your literacy curriculum; they support close reading and thorough understanding.

However, we can't systematically evaluate student performance on every one of these questions. We need to identify priorities. You may want to customize the list for your population of students, but the following are questions I would be sure to assess:

- *Standard 1: Which two details support the conclusion _____?*

Ask this question when your text includes multiple pieces of evidence, and make sure your students can locate more than one detail.

- *Standard 2: Which sentence best describes the lesson (theme, main idea, etc.)?*

If you include the identification of theme as a regular part of your literacy routine, students will become more adept at identifying a central idea—especially if you begin at DOK 2 by recognizing a theme rather than producing one.

- *Standard 2: Which sentences belong in a summary? Which should be left out? or What is the best summary?*

Once again, at this Depth of Knowledge, the challenge is to understand what makes a good summary, not to produce one. Elementary students will see this question on assessments frequently.

- *Standard 3: Arrange the events from the passage in order.*

Don't underestimate the importance of recognizing how events unfold in either informational or literary passages. This is a prerequisite to understanding cause and effect.

- *Standard 3: Which event [initiates the rising action] of the excerpt?*

It could be any plot element. At the primary level, begin by asking students to identify story parts (characters, setting, problem, events, solution). Recognizing story parts or plot elements is nonnegotiable as the foundation for deeper comprehension.

- *Standard 4: Part A: What is the meaning of [calamity] in paragraph 7? Part B: What clue in the article supports this meaning?*

We can engage students in conversation about word meanings very naturally as we teach. We ask, "What is the meaning of _____?" and then ask, "How did you know?" Because assessment items that measure vocabulary will likely follow this two-part format, we should include similar items on our classroom assessments. Here's the challenge: Make sure the word you select has a contextual clue within the passage. Also make sure you include some figurative phrases, not just single words.

- *Standard 5: What is the overall structure of this [article]?*

Remember to ask this question, and especially remember to ask it about different text structures.

- *Standard 5: What kind of information is the author giving us in this part of the [article]?*

This question and others that relate to the internal structure of a text will be important to students' success on new assessments. If you include questions about internal structure on your assessments, you'll be more likely to include this in your instruction, too.

- *Standard 7: Which idea from the [article] is supported by the [photograph]?*

In texts for older readers, the illustrations support the content rather than mimic it. Make sure students understand this distinction.

- *Standard 8: What kind of evidence does the author provide to support the point that _____?*

As discussed earlier in this chapter, we need to be more intentional about teaching with texts that represent different kinds of evidence.

Writing standards: *Choose the best [beginning, ending, supporting] paragraph for this [story].*

Before students can write a worthy beginning, ending, or any other part of a narrative or informational piece, they need to recognize what constitutes good writing. Show students different beginnings or other parts of a story and ask, "Which one do you like best? Why?"

It will be important to make smart decisions about what to assess for the rigor of DOK 2 for two reasons. First, we need to be sure students can demonstrate thinking at this level before moving on to DOK 3, which builds on this foundation. Second, we want to be sure we've covered *all* standards. To that end, I've supplied a Data Collection Chart for Skills (Figure 7.23) on page 189 in Chapter 7. It will help you keep track of who has made progress in which areas, and which students need reteaching of skills.

Bottom Line for Aligning Rigor and Formative Assessment for DOK 2: There are many skill-based questions we can ask for Depth of Knowledge 2, and we may ask all of them from time to time in our instruction. But for assessment, narrow the field a bit to what is most important to your students and their needs. This list of priority questions may change throughout the year and may be different for different students in your class.

3

Strategic Reasoning: Supporting Depth of Knowledge 3

With Depth of Knowledge 3, we enter the realm of complex thinking. Let's begin by considering the underlying principles of this level and its associated rigor (see Figure 3.1).

FIGURE 3.1 | **Depth of Knowledge 3 and Rigor**

Depth of Knowledge 3	**The Rigor**
Employing strategic thinking and reasoning	Insight into content and craft based on depth of reasoning

Underlying Principles: Rigor for DOK 3

The criteria for both Depth of Knowledge 3 ("employing strategic thinking and reasoning") and the rigor of this Depth of Knowledge ("insight into content and craft based on depth of reasoning") are a bit mysterious at first glance. Just what do we mean by "strategic thinking and reasoning"? What counts as "insight into content and craft"?

The best way to begin to understand the rigor of DOK 3 is to view it in comparison to DOK 2. Whereas DOK 2 typically yields a single right answer, DOK 3 often generates divergent thinking and more than one possible answer. The second Depth of Knowledge relies primarily on text evidence for responses, whereas the third asks students to think more abstractly, going deeper into the text by using logic as well as evidence. Although tasks at both levels involve a process for deciding *how* to answer, DOK 3 also asks students to explain their thinking, the reasoning behind their response. This is what we mean by "strategic reasoning."

Strategies Reimagined

We need to clarify some language here. Back in the day—not so very long ago, actually—the word *strategies*, when applied to comprehension, referred to a repertoire of metacognitive processes such as visualizing, making personal connections, and synthesizing (Boyles, 2004). Those processes continue to be useful tools to gain meaning from a text: *What do you picture here? Has something like this ever happened to you?* But "strategic reasoning" in the context of Depth of Knowledge is more about how you puzzle through a text, putting all the pieces together until you can see the big picture.

You read like a *reader*, mining nuances of meaning; and you read like a *writer*, discerning why the author crafted a text in particular ways. How deep are your insights? That's what DOK 3 tasks are designed to measure. Yes, questions at this level are harder. But truth to tell, they are also more fun.

The Hard Fun of DOK 3

Consider the wisdom of Seymour Papert (1999): "We learn best and we work best if we enjoy what we are doing. But fun and enjoying doesn't mean 'easy.' The best fun is hard fun."

What kind of "hard fun" can we offer up in the design of literacy tasks? Let's be honest: most of what we ask students to do at the first two Depths of Knowledge does not qualify as "fun." For example, you ask, "Can you find two details that show that the mother was motivated to steal the apples because her children were hungry?" Competent readers know to return to the text to retrieve the requisite details, though this may signal more of a robotic obligation than a passion for self-expression.

Now let's try out a question that builds on the application of a concept: "In your opinion, are the mother's actions more justified once you understand what motivated her? Make an inference about her motivation, and explain your reasoning based on events in the story." Now there's a question kids can sink their teeth into. Why?

Although this question is challenging, students also find it "fun" because their thinking matters. They need the same textual details as in the first question. But to answer the second query well, they must go deeper into the text, generating a response that may be different from that of their peers because they get to consider the problem from their unique vantage point. This "hard fun" is the essence of Depth of Knowledge 3, and it plays a central role in new standards-based assessments—it's *that* important.

We can have lots of hard fun with Depth of Knowledge 3. Let's look at the rigor that new assessments are expecting.

Measuring DOK 3 on Standards-Based Assessments

The first issue at hand is the number of items at this Depth of Knowledge. Remember from Chapter 1 that past assessments focused only minimally on DOK 3. By contrast, new standards-based assessments include approximately the same proportion of DOK 2 as DOK 3 items, which is a sizable shift. Remember, too, that *all* DOK 3 items ask students to explain their thinking. In the list of sample items shown in Figure 3.2, that part of the question is not repeated for each item.

Aligning Rigor and Standards for DOK 3

The questions in Figure 3.2 are the kind of items that are likely to appear on new standards-based assessments. However, many additional questions for Depth of Knowledge 3 could be asked within our instruction. Those questions will be featured later in this chapter when we examine the implications of DOK 3 for close reading. For now, let's focus only on the items in the list in the figure.

Standards Emphasized for DOK 3

Apart from Standard 1, with its emphasis on evidence only, all standards are emphasized at this Depth of Knowledge. Hence, rather than looking at individual standards, it's more important to look at trends across all standards.

You perhaps noticed a few key points right away. First, and perhaps most important of all, every DOK 3 task demands inferential thinking. Sometimes this language will be right in the question: *Make an inference about* _____. Other times, students will be asked to *draw a conclusion about* _____, which is essentially the same thing. It's possible that other language will be used, too. But regardless, it's all about the inference (or conclusion).

Other common Depth of Knowledge 3 expectations for students will be to do the following:

- Determine importance
- Recognize relationships
- Make qualitative judgments—for example, what is *best* or *most likely*
- Think like the author (or narrator or character)
- Examine the development of ideas
- Explain *why* or *how*
- Construct responses, in addition to responding to multiple-choice questions

FIGURE 3.2 | Sample Assessment Items for DOK 3

Reading Standard 1: Textual evidence
· Which details are the most surprising? Why? · Which details are the most important? Why? · Why do you think the author included these details?

Reading Standard 2: Development of central ideas
· What is the theme (or main idea) of the passage? Use details from the passage to support your answer. (Could also ask for multiple main ideas or themes.) · What conclusions can be drawn based on the paragraph? Select two conclusions from the list below. · How did the author develop the theme (or central idea) of _____ in this [poem]? · What inference can be made about [Annie Sullivan, based on her work with Helen Keller]? · What conclusion can be drawn about the author's point of view about [school uniforms] based on information in this article?

Reading Standard 3: Story/text components and relationship among story parts or parts of an informational text
· Which of these conclusions about [character/person] is supported by the passage? · How might this story be different if told from _____'s point of view? · How does the characters' relationship develop throughout the text? · In what ways is the [problem] in this story related to the [setting]? Choose all statements that apply. · What conclusion can be drawn about [the problem] from details in the text? · Which of these inferences about the [character's/person's attitude—or motivation] is supported in the text? · What does the information in this [article] show about the author's point of view about [living in the woods]? · How do the characters' actions show their relationship in the story? · In your opinion, what was the turning point of this [story/situation]?

Reading Standard 4: Vocabulary in context
· Why did the author most likely use the underlined phrase? (What is the [metaphor] showing?) · Why did the author [write the word FIRE in a larger font with all uppercase letters]? · Explain how the author's choice of words [in this advertisement] helps to convince [buyers] that [they will want to purchase this product]. · Choose the sentence that fits logically into the story and best maintains the [narrator's] tone. · What does the use of the [word/figurative phrase] suggest about _____? · What effect does the author create by using the phrase _____? · What does the phrase _____ tell the reader about [character]?

Reading Standard 5: Text features, structure, and genre
· What is the most likely reason the author included [a graph of _____]? · How does this [text feature] add to your understanding of _____? · What is the **most likely** reason the author used a [cause-and-effect structure] in the passage?

FIGURE 3.2 | (continued)

· Why is including [description] important to understanding this passage?

· Why do you think the author chose to write about [sharks] in the form of a [poem]?

· How does the [third paragraph] add to your understanding of the [problem]?

Reading Standard 6: Point of view and purpose

· What inference can be made about the [character's/person's] feelings about _____?

· What conclusion about the author's point of view is supported by the passage?

· Why do you think the author [begins this article with a quote]?

· What was the author's purpose for including [the sentence about _____]?

· Which of these inferences best support the author's purpose in writing this [article]?

Reading Standard 7: Illustrations and other nonprint sources

· How does [the chart] add to your understanding of _____?

· What were the author's most likely reasons for including [the map] in the passage?

· Why is using a [timeline] important to understanding the information in the passage?

Reading Standard 8: Use of evidence and reasoning

· Which details from [the text] **best** support [the argument that _____]?

· Which details from the text are irrelevant to the author's claim that _____?

· What additional evidence could the author have included to make his argument more convincing?

· What point does the author of the article support with at least two pieces of evidence?

· What do you think is the most convincing (or best) evidence in support of the author's claim? Why?

· What did the author intend by mentioning _____?

Reading Standard 9: Text connections

· Explain why _____. Use two details from Source 1 and two details from Source 2.

· [Source 1] gives information about _____. Choose **two** facts from [Source 2] that could add to your understanding from Source 1.

· Match each source with the detail that is included in that source.

· Each source explains _____. Use **one example** from Source 1 and **one example** from Source 3 to support your explanation. For each example, include the source title and number.

· Source 3 includes information about _____. Explain how this information could be helpful if it were added to Source 2. Give **two** examples from Source 2 to support your explanation.

· Which element specific to [historical fiction] do [Source 1] and [Source 2] have in common? Explain.

· Explain how each [tall tale] could be improved by including more [tall tale] elements.

· Which detail in [Source 1] is most relevant to the argument in [Source 2]?

· Which of the [three] sources would be most helpful for explaining _____?

· What point of view is expressed in each passage?

· Based on the features of [an adventure story], which features do you find in [Source 1]? Which features do you find in [Source 2]?

(continued)

FIGURE 3.2 | (continued)

· Which source provides better information about _____?
· Which source is more convincing?
· Does the author of [Source 2] do a good job of convincing you that _____? Give at least two details from that source.

Writing: Revising and editing for organization, elaboration, and clarity
· Write an introduction to this writing piece that states your opinion.
· Write an introduction that clearly states the main idea and sets up the information to come.
· Write an introduction to this story that establishes the setting and introduces the main character and the problem.
· Revise [paragraph 6] of this story to include more narrative elements such as dialogue and description.
· Use the student's notes to write a paragraph that adds more facts to support [paragraph 3].
· Write an ending to the narrative that follows logically from the events.
· Write an introduction that establishes a clear claim that supports _____. (Grade 8)

The Format of DOK 3 Items

Noting that a key element at this Depth of Knowledge is asking students to explain their thinking—*why* they believe their answer is correct—it would seem DOK 3 is better suited to questions with a constructed response rather than a multiple-choice format. But that's not always true. Although *some* reasoning can't be assessed by multiple-choice items (also called selected responses), it works well for other items (see http://ctf2point0.weebly.com/selected-response .html).

For example, the question might ask: *Which two conclusions about the impact of global warming are supported in the text?* Six options are provided, and students need to activate their inferential reasoning skills to make their selections. Here's another possibility: *Which statement best shows how the story would have been different if it had been told from the grandmother's point of view?* Here, students need to infer how a narrator's perspective influences how a story unfolds.

There are abundant examples of selected-response items that measure DOK 3 on standards-based assessments, which could be considered both a strength and a weakness. On the plus side, we're not attempting to measure students' capacity to read by their writing proficiency, as we do when the question requires a constructed response. On the other hand, students need to be able to articulate their reasoning if they intend to apply critical thinking skills to solve real problems outside the classroom. Hence, some DOK 3 assessment items are designed to examine the way readers put their thinking into words.

Consider this example: *What conclusion can be drawn about the author's point of view about wolves? Use details from the article in your response.* Now we get to see not only how insightful the student is, but how well she can communicate those insights. It's the ability to communicate thinking that makes reasoning useful. Expressing ideas is also what makes thinking fun.

There's something exhilarating about having an opinion and sharing it. You choose just the right details and just the right words to convey your ideas effectively. And if you do a good job, your audience is convinced—another reason why DOK 3 tasks qualify as hard fun—though it's safe to say that "fun" won't be the first word that comes to mind when students see some of these assessment questions.

Academic Language and Graphic Support for DOK 3

Depth of Knowledge 3 underscores additional complexities in academic language and in the kinds of supports we can provide students to make language accessible. As the expected rigor goes deeper, questions become more complex. Sometimes the issue is not multiple labels for the same concept, but too many words that require translation all at once.

Here's a 6th grade item: *Which plot event is the first to contribute significantly to the folktale's resolution?* (McGraw-Hill, 2015c, p. 5). Students need to integrate the words *plot, contribute, folktale,* and *resolution.* It's a lot to digest, and what students really need to navigate items like this is practice—not practice answering the question, but practice paraphrasing the question.

Go to any site where you can find released assessment items that mimic the kinds of questions students are likely to see on new assessments. (Several sites are listed on page 198, at the end of Chapter 7, Teaching Tools and Resources.) The following question is a 4th grade item and comes from STAAR, the assessment students take in Texas (tea.texas.gov/WorkArea/DownloadAsset.aspx?id =51539609632):

> The author included the simile in paragraph 13 to suggest that Pacy's school vacations —
>
> F are no longer fun for her
> G have gotten longer
> H allow her time to play with her sisters
> J make her think of her friends

Sometimes when you share potential assessment items with your students, it's good to include answer options as well, to demonstrate how to approach the elimination of incorrect responses. For any question, have students identify the key words—in this case, *simile, paragraph, suggest.* Can they explain what the question is asking in their own words? With so many samples available, choose items at or near grade level for realistic views of the language your students are likely to see.

Helping students cope with the language of questions will improve their ability to demonstrate understanding across all standards. But there are additional ways we can increase the odds for student success at the DOK 3 level by tweaking our instruction, standard by standard.

Where to Increase Instructional Focus for DOK 3

At DOK 3, almost every potential question reveals an opportunity for increased rigor. Here are a few highlights.

Standard 1

- *Which details are the most surprising? Why?*

This is an excellent question to help students monitor their understanding. If they're always looking for a possible surprise, they'll stay tuned in. At the same time, they'll recognize what's important because when an author catches you off-guard, the detail is usually worth remembering.

Standard 2

- *What inference can be made [about Annie Sullivan based on her work with Helen Keller]?*
- *What conclusion can be drawn about the author's point of view about [school uniforms] based on information in this article?*

Many, many Standard 2 questions will focus on inferring the text's central idea, although sometimes these items won't *look* like central-idea questions. The question about Annie Sullivan appears to be about a *person*, thus related to Standard 3 (text components). The school-uniforms item asks about point of view. So, isn't this Standard 6 (point of view)? Not really.

Look again at these two questions and you'll see that both are really probing the main idea: the reason for Annie's success with Helen, and the writer's ratio-nale for or against school uniforms. Standard 2 questions can be tricky because they do not always scream *theme*. Help students recognize when the question is, in fact, addressing the big idea in the text—even when the task doesn't mention *theme* or one of its substitute terms. Note that sometimes items within other standards will ask for an inference, too. It could be an inference about a person, a problem, or just about anything.

Essential for DOK 3 rigor is making sure that you talk about theme (or main idea) for every text your students read. Begin looking for this big idea (or mul-tiple big ideas) from the very first paragraph so students can see that a theme is a thread of meaning that runs through the entire work and the author starts developing it right away.

Finally, don't stop with simply *finding* the theme. Make sure students can explain how the author developed it, and why, in real life, this theme/main idea is so important. We'll cover more about this when we get to the formative assess-ment of DOK 3, later in this chapter.

Standard 3

- *How might this story be different if told from _____'s point of view?*

Here's another instance where the question *asks* about point of view, but now the focus is on understanding character. Students will be successful responding to a question of this sort if you move on from character basics like traits and feelings to motivations, attitudes, relationships, and character development.

- *How do the characters' actions show their relationship in the story?*

If you reread Standard 3, you will see that the essence is for students to recognize the *relationship* between textual elements, which is precisely the focus of this question. On page 181 in Chapter 7, you'll find an anchor chart, Words That Describe Character Relationships (Figure 7.18). It can get your students thinking about how characters in a story (or people in an informational article) relate to and interact with each other. Are they supportive? Hostile? Antagonistic? Something else? But hanging this chart on your classroom wall will not be enough. You'll also need to talk with your students about the meaning of these words and the kinds of behavior that define each one.

Standard 4

- *What effect does the author create by using the phrase _____?*
- *What does the phrase _____ tell the reader about [character/person]?*

A highlight of Standard 4 (vocabulary) for Depth of Knowledge 3 is the emphasis on word choice and how the author's use of words contributes to the tone or effect of a piece of writing. I think we can make the biggest difference in this area just by training ourselves to pause when we come upon a strong word in the text and taking the time to reflect with students: *Why do you think the author chose this word? What does it show about the author's attitude toward _____?*

In the second sample question, readers need to recognize not just the *tone* of the word, but also its implications for understanding the character: *What does the phrase "jumpy as a flea" tell you about this person?* We need to be more intentional about looking for teachable moments to contemplate tone as we're reading any text. You'll be amazed at the words and phrases that leap off the page once you're aware of what to look for. Here's a sample from the *Black Beauty* passage used in Chapter 5 of this book (the complete text of *Black Beauty* is available at http://www.gutenberg.org/files/271/271.txt) for the close reading lessons, where Ginger, Beauty's companion, is explaining to him what her early life was like:

> Several men came to catch me, and when at last they closed me in at one corner of the field, one caught me by the forelock, another caught me by the nose and held it so tight I could hardly draw my breath; then another

took my under jaw in his hard hand and wrenched my mouth open, and so by force they got on the halter and the bar into my mouth; then one dragged me along by the halter, another flogging behind, and this was the first experience I had of men's kindness; it was all force.

We can first ask students to identify the strong words. They may respond with these: *catch, closed me in, held it so tight, could hardly draw my breath, wrenched my mouth open, force, dragged, flogging.* Answering this question accurately is a good DOK 2 task. But it's our next question, for DOK 3, that matters most: *What tone is the author creating here, and how do you think she feels about Ginger's treatment?*

Standard 5

- *What is the most likely reason the author included [a graph of _____]?*
- *Why do you think the author chose to write about [sharks] in the form of a [poem]?*
- *What is the most likely reason the author used a [cause-and-effect structure] in the passage?*
- *How does this [text feature] add to your understanding of _____ ?*
- *What is the best reason the author chose to begin this story with [a conversation]?*

You will need to fasten your seatbelt for Standard 5 (text features and structure) because this standard promises to be a wild ride for Depth of Knowledge 3. As noted in Chapter 2, about Depth of Knowledge 2, much of the focus on text structure will be uncharted territory for many students. And now at Depth of Knowledge 3, the questions are even more demanding—with the likelihood of several DOK 3 items for this standard appearing on new assessments at any grade level.

As seen in the questions above, structure can be viewed from many perspectives—the inclusion of text features like graphs; the genre chosen by the author; the organizational framework, such as cause and effect; and literary elements used, such as conversation. To respond to these questions, readers will be asked to "think like the author." They will be asked to consider how a structural feature adds to their understanding. Students will not be able to answer questions such as these if the first time they see them is on assessments.

Model your thinking as you talk about text: *I think the author may have started this article with a conversation to show that people have very different opinions about year-round school. He wanted us to see that these individuals disagreed strongly, and they each had their reasons.* Then ask your students to weigh in: *What do you think?* With more opportunities to think deeply about text structure, students will begin to understand how to approach these questions.

Standard 6

- *What inference can be made about the [character's/person's] feelings about _____?*
- *What conclusion about the author's point of view is supported by the passage?*
- *What was the author's purpose for including [the sentence about _____]?*

There are a few highlights worth noting for Standard 6 items. First, remember that this standard is not represented below Depth of Knowledge 3, so all questions students see aligned to this standard will expect deep thinking—for example, understanding that a character's *feelings* reflect the character's point of view. Also, students will be challenged to discern the *author's* point of view, which is often subtler than the point of view of a fictional narrator.

Especially significant is a new expectation for author's *purpose*. Students have gotten too complacent about what *purpose* means. They barely look at a text before announcing: *The purpose of a story is to entertain; expository writing is to inform; opinion writing is to persuade.* These automatic responses will not get the job done on new assessments. Look at the following item from a 4th grade STAAR test:

What is the author's primary purpose in writing the letter?

A. To explain why dogs are better behaved if they are used to being around people

B. To share information about a potential volunteer opportunity at the Medway dog park

C. To suggest that many dog owners do not give their pets an opportunity to exercise

D. To convince the town council that the citizens of Medway would benefit from a dog park

It is clear from this item that recognizing the author's purpose will require a thoughtful analysis: When the author wrote this letter, what was she hoping the outcome would be? Our instruction should press for this deeper reasoning, as well. If the letter was to persuade, persuade about *what*? *How* did the author make her argument convincing?

Share books with students that may not fit their rote definition of author's purpose. I finished reading *Turtle, Turtle, Watch Out!* by April Pulley Sayre to a class of 2nd graders. "That was a nice story," one of the students announced as I closed the book. "Yes, it was," I agreed, "but do you think the author wrote this book just to tell us a nice story?" "Well, I think she wanted us to know sea turtles are in danger and we can all help save them." This 2nd grade friend was right; this "nice story" had a purpose beyond entertainment.

A final observation about this standard is that many assessment items focus on the purpose of a part of a text rather than the whole text. When the question asks, "What is the author's purpose for including paragraph 2?" we should go back and scrutinize that paragraph and the ones preceding and following it. We need to figure out not just the information it contains, but why the author wanted us to have this information and how it contributes to the text as a whole. These are the kinds of questions that will get kids thinking!

Standard 7

- *How does [the chart] add to your understanding of _____?*
- *What were the author's most likely reasons for including [the map] in the passage?*

Standard 7, with its emphasis on nonprint text, does not play a major role in new assessments right now, though this may change as more states move to online tests where there's greater opportunity to include video, audio, and full-color images like photographs and artwork. For now, many of the images students will see, other than text features like maps and charts, will be illustrations or black-and-white photographs accompanying a text.

As with the questions for Standard 6, students will again be charged with deciding how an image adds to their understanding or why the author may have included it. We have a clear pattern of questions from standard to standard, especially at this third Depth of Knowledge. Asking these questions in our literacy instruction will help students succeed not just as test-takers but as thinkers.

Standard 8

- *Which details from [the text] **best** support [the argument that _____]?*
- *Which details from the text are irrelevant to the author's claim that _____?*

Because Standard 8 is not addressed below DOK 3, this will be students' first experience with critical analysis of text to judge the sufficiency and relevance of evidence. Remember that this standard applies only to informational text, so ask your Standard 8 questions for nonfiction. Clarify the words *relevant* and *irrelevant*. For any author's claim, ask your students what they consider the *best* (or strongest) evidence, and then have them explain their reasoning.

Although it's not likely to be a test item, I also like to ask, "What do you think the author could have explained more clearly to help you understand it better?" It's important for readers to realize that sometimes their lack of comprehension is more a function of the author's writing than their thinking.

Standard 9

- *Explain why _____. Use two details from Source 1 and two details from Source 2.*
- *Which element specific to [historical fiction] do [Source 1] and [Source 2] have in common? Explain.*

- *Which source is more convincing?*
- *Source 3 includes information about _____. Explain how this information can be helpful if it were added to Source 2. Give two examples from Source 2 to support your explanation.*

The focus of Standard 9 is making connections between texts. Text connections are often considered the domain of Depth of Knowledge 4 because using texts together is a defining feature of performance tasks. When students write a story, a full essay, or a research report of several pages, doing so *will* require DOK 4, which will be discussed at length in the next chapter. However, questions that focus on a specific task and may be answered using a multiple-choice format, or in a paragraph, are usually considered DOK 3.

The most basic observation about Standard 9 questions is that items will call for many kinds of connections. The most rudimentary expectation, as noted in the first bullet item, will be for students to use information from all (two or three) sources to answer a question. Many of these questions will simultaneously address other standards, such as the one above that requires genre knowledge (Standard 5), and the item asking which source is more convincing (Standard 8). A more sophisticated challenge will be for students to recognize how information from one source could enhance another source.

Writing standards

- *Write an introduction that clearly states the main idea and sets up the information to come. (Grade 4)*
- *Revise [paragraph 6] of this story to include more narrative elements such as dialogue and description.*
- *Use the student's notes to write a paragraph that adds more facts to support [paragraph 3].*

Notice first that the rigor of Depth of Knowledge 3 for Writing standards asks students to focus on *parts* of a text, rather than writing full texts. This alone should be a major takeaway for teachers: all writing instruction does not need to culminate in a whole published story, essay, or any other kind of writing. By contrast, there should be lots of lessons on the crafting of specific parts of a writing piece.

This approach might apply to any mode of writing—opinion/argument, informative/explanatory, or narrative—and could focus on the introduction to the piece, a body paragraph, or its conclusion. Recognizing crafted elements under each writing trait, explained in the previous chapter for connecting reading and writing at Depth of Knowledge 2, will be a critical first step. Teaching students to *apply* these crafts in their own writing will be the challenge for writing at Depth of Knowledge 3.

For opinion/argument and informative/explanatory writing (Writing Standards 1 and 2), the expectations are clear for the organization and elaboration

All writing instruction does not need to culminate in a whole published story, essay, or any other kind of writing.

(development) of a writing piece, especially for grades 3 and above, where the standard is divided into several substandards. We look at those standards and we can imagine the instruction for each part of the piece: beginning, middle, and end. But for narrative writing, there's a greater disconnect between what we want the outcome to be and our plan for helping students get there. We can't divide a narrative text into neatly segmented parts the way we can with informational or opinion writing. In support of well-developed narrative writing, a high-impact strategy is described later in this chapter under Connecting Reading and Writing.

> **Bottom Line for Aligning Rigor and Standards for DOK 3:** When we say that new standards are hard or assessments that measure new standards are hard, what we are recognizing is that these standards now assess knowledge at a deeper level than students have experienced in the past. We can help our students succeed at this Depth of Knowledge first by making sure we include DOK 3 questions for all standards in our literacy instruction.

Aligning Rigor and Text Complexity for DOK 3

Different kinds of thinking call for different kinds of texts. For Depth of Knowledge 1, we talked about choosing resources that keep kids engaged, so they'll be motivated to pursue evidence. For DOK 2, we focused on texts that were a good match for different standards. Now we come to Depth of Knowledge 3, where the challenge is to select resources students will want to discuss. What kinds of text might be worthy of discussion?

Students will be eager to talk about texts that are ambiguous, provocative, or personally or emotionally challenging (Strong, Silver, & Perini, 2001). If teachers selected reading material for students based on these criteria, I expect there would be many more lively conversations in classrooms. And out of those conversations, as students probed texts deeply, would come great insights—exactly what we're seeking for the rigor of DOK 3.

Let's look at what we mean by *ambiguous, provocative,* and *personally or emotionally challenging,* and texts that might qualify for each category. These sources, all from the Bibliography of Student Resources at the end of this book, were selected to provide opportunities for deep thinking.

Meaning That Is Ambiguous

Ambiguous doesn't mean "confusing." Precisely what we do *not* want is a roomful of confused kids. More to the point, ambiguous texts may include more than one way of looking at a situation; the message might be interpreted in multiple ways. There could be different criteria for deciding, or different points of view. Perhaps the story is an allegory in which the central idea is not immediately clear. Or the author leads the reader down a familiar path—and then switches it up for a surprise ending. It could be a mystery in which readers collect clues along the way and must distinguish them from the "red herrings" thrown in for extra intrigue. Or it could be a matter of opinion, based on the sufficiency of evidence. Students will sustain interest in these texts because they must piece together clues to make meaning. It's the messiness that holds their attention.

Ambiguous texts for grades K–2 students

- *Eggbert*, **by Tom Ross (picture book)**, is an allegory that requires students to unravel meaning.
- **"The New Kid on the Block" (poem), by Jack Prelutsky**, in *The New Kid on the Block*, has a surprise at the end.
- **"The Wind" (poem), by James Reeves**, provides clues to solve a riddle.
- **"Should You Be Afraid of Sharks?" (ReadWorks)** presents surprising but true facts.
- **"World Wonders" (ReadWorks)** offers the opportunity to choose a personal favorite among world wonders.

Ambiguous texts for grades 3–5 students

- *Voices in the Park*, **by Anthony Browne**, tells the same story from four points of view.
- **"Farewell" (speech), by Lou Gehrig**, is an example of a person facing reality with a commendable but unlikely perspective.
- **"Spaghetti" (short story), by Cynthia Rylant**, in *Every Living Thing*, serves up many unanswered questions to ponder.
- **"Your Name in Gold" (short story), by A. F. Bauman**, in *Chicken Soup for the Kid's Soul*, ends with a surprise that readers might (or might not) see coming.

Ambiguous texts for grades 6–8 students

- *Encounter*, **by Jane Yolen**, shows how unsettling it can be to view historical "facts" from a different perspective.
- *The Wretched Stone*, **by Chris Van Allsburg**, will have readers synthesizing clues to make an inference.
- *The Three Questions: Based on a Story by Leo Tolstoy*, **by Jon Muth**, is an allegory that begs readers to consider how *they* would answer these same three questions.

- "Battle over the Pledge" (ReadWorks) underscores the value of understanding both sides of an issue before taking a stand.
- *Yertle the Turtle*, by Dr. Seuss, is not just a story for little kids but a book with allegorical implications for big kids, too.

Meaning That Is Provocative

Meaning that is provocative is often derived from texts that address life's "big issues"—the atrocities of the Holocaust, slavery, or child labor, to name a few. Provocative text could involve making a difficult decision, cause you to question your values, or involve an ethical or moral choice. This is the stuff that people feel so passionate about that they can hardly wait to make their voice heard, take a stand, or act.

Sometimes, when the big issue is a current one—something that's in the news—students hear commentary at home that may define their position. But often it's their child-size sense of justice and dignity that prevails. There are texts of all descriptions that speak to big issues—from chapter books to picture books, informational articles, speeches, even poetry. Some are true, and others are based on what's true. If you want to have a great discussion, start with a provocative topic.

Provocative texts for grades K–2 students

- *Last Stop on Market Street*, by Matt de la Peña—Big question: Whose responsibility is it to feed the poor?
- *Something Beautiful*, by Sharon Denis Wyeth—Big question: Where can we find beauty in our world when beauty does not seem to surround us?
- *Never Smile at a Monkey*, by Steve Jenkins—Big question: Why is it important to behave responsibly around wild animals?
- "Meet Rosa Parks" (ReadWorks)—Big question: How do we resist authority respectfully?
- *Turtle, Turtle, Watch Out!* by April Pulley Sayre—Big question: How do we protect an endangered animal?
- *Peppe the Lamplighter*, by Elisa Bartone—Big question: What makes a job important?

Provocative texts for grades 3–5 students

- *Mercedes and the Chocolate Pilot: A True Story of the Berlin Airlift and the Candy That Dropped from the Sky*, by Margot Theis Raven—Big question: How do we find hope amid destruction?
- *Freedom Summer*, by Deborah Wiles—Big question: What is the impact of discrimination?
- "Ballad of Birmingham" (poem), by Dudley Randall—Big question: Who are the victims of prejudice?

- *Martin's Big Words*, **by Doreen Rappaport**—Big question: How do we fight for change in a positive way?
- **"A Tale of Segregation: Fetching Water" (ReadWorks)**—Big question: How can we stand up for the dignity of all people?

Provocative texts for grades 6–8 students

- *14 Cows for America*, **by Carmen Agra Deedy**—Big question: What does empathy look like?
- *Remember: The Journey to School Integration*, **by Toni Morrison**—Big question: What is the impact of racism?
- **"World War II Posters" (ReadWorks)**—Big question: How do images reveal a culture's values?
- *My Secret Camera: Life in a Lodz Ghetto*, **photographs by Mendel Grossman; text by Frank Dabba Smith**—Big question: How could the world let something as horrific as concentration camps happen?
- **"Letter from Jackie Robinson on Civil Rights" (ReadWorks)**—Big question: How do we ensure the civil rights of all people?
- **"Japanese Internment Camps: A Personal Account" (ReadWorks)**—Big question: What can our country learn from its mistakes?
- *Oh, Rats! The Story of Rats and People*, **by Albert Marrin**—Big question: What do we do about rodent infestation?

Meaning That Is Personally or Emotionally Challenging

We're hardly strangers to the idea of connecting personally to text. In fact, the past couple of decades have witnessed what many now consider an over-emphasis on text-to-self connections. The intent was a good one: read books on topics that are relatable and then focus on what makes the subject personally meaningful. Where this went off track, I think, was that the connection remained focused on what happened in the reader's *past* rather than how it might affect life going forward.

Let's suppose the book was about bullying, certainly an issue of personal challenge that affects many students. Kids (and teachers) got caught up in conversations about who had been bullied, how this made them feel, and the details of those experiences. A more productive way to go might have been to acknowledge the past but then quickly move on to the future: How could the experience of the character in this book make a difference to you the next time you are bullied or when you see someone else bullied?

Making a powerful personal connection means connecting to the message. This is what makes reading transformative. Texts with the potential to have an impact on personal growth might focus on making good choices, the importance of a character trait, making a mature decision, or putting others before ourselves.

Personally or emotionally challenging texts for grades K–2 students

- *Stand Tall, Molly Lou Mellon*, by Patty Lovell, is about dealing with bullies.
- *Amazing Grace*, by Mary Hoffman, is about dealing with discrimination based on gender and race.
- *Those Shoes*, by Maribeth Boelts, is about making the distinction between wants and needs.
- *Down the Road*, by Alice Schertle, is about making choices and accepting consequences.
- *The Goose That Laid the Golden Eggs*, an Aesop's Fable, is about being happy with what we have.
- *The Sandwich Swap*, by Queen Rania of Jordan Al Abdullah, is about appreciating someone else's point of view and trying something new.

Personally or emotionally challenging texts for grades 3–5 students

- *The Summer My Father Was Ten*, by Pat Brisson, is about taking responsibility for our actions.
- "Mother to Son" (poem), by Langston Hughes, is about perseverance in the face of challenges.
- *More Than Anything Else*, by Marie Bradby, is about following our dreams.
- "Spaghetti" (short story), by Cynthia Rylant, in *Every Living Thing*, is about everyone needing a friend.
- "Big Dreams" (ReadWorks) is about setting personal goals.
- *The Can Man*, by Laura Williams, is about thinking of others' needs before our own.

Personally or emotionally challenging texts for grades 6–8 students

- *Fox*, by Margaret Wild, is about distinguishing between real and "fake" friends.
- "Still I Rise" (poem), by Maya Angelou, is about overcoming obstacles to achieve our dreams.
- "Taking Down the Green-Eyed Monster" (Read Works) is about dealing with jealousy.
- *The Fun They Had*, by Isaac Asimov, warns us to be careful about what we wish for.

Bottom Line for Aligning Rigor and Text Complexity for DOK 3: Because this Depth of Knowledge invites students to contemplate controversial topics, or topics that can be viewed from more than one perspective, we need to choose resources that lend themselves to conversation. Choosing texts that are ambiguous, provocative, or personally or emotionally challenging will offer students a wide range of literary vistas to explore.

Aligning Rigor and Close Reading for DOK 3

The rigor of Depth of Knowledge 3 is our strongest reason thus far for teaching students to read closely. We need texts that are ambiguous, provocative, and personally or emotionally challenging to ask those weighty questions that lead students to profound insights. Our goal is insight, based on strategic reasoning. But what's the plan to get there?

Unlike the one-step process of returning to the text to find evidence—the close reading go-to strategy for DOK 1—and the multistep, gradual-release process for building skills featured for DOK 2, there is no actual process for approaching DOK 3, no set of steps to follow.

No steps to follow? This situation makes us nervous. Our teacher playbook is filled with best practices that have nice-and-neat procedures. We implement the procedures well, with a little tweaking here and there, and our students achieve. But DOK 3 is all about logic. We perhaps could teach them the rules of formal argument, or stage a debate—which might work for older students and which we could implement occasionally in the classroom. But we need a way to engage students in logical thought regularly and often (every day!). And the approach needs to work for little kids as well as big kids.

The solution is simpler and more straightforward than you might think. What all students need, and what will make the biggest difference, is *exposure*. Yes, exposure! Students need to hear DOK 3 questions. They need to hear their teachers modeling logical thinking. And they need to experiment with logical thinking of their own.

It's a matter of asking the follow-up question, the one that moves the needle from an answer with essentially one correct response, to a response with many possibilities. For the most part, DOK 3 questions bear a strong resemblance to DOK 2 items, now "kicked up" to require strategic reasoning, beyond the retrieval of basic evidence or the application of a skill.

DOK 3 questions bear a strong resemblance to DOK 2 items, now "kicked up" to require strategic reasoning.

Moving from DOK 2 to DOK 3

For DOK 2, we ask students to name the character trait displayed by Anna and Caleb in the early part of Patricia MacLachlan's *Sarah, Plain and Tall*, when those two characters are contemplating Sarah's arrival. The children are afraid Sarah will not like them, and so probable answers will be *nervous, cautious, worried*, or another term with about the same meaning. In a very limited way, these responses could be considered divergent because the words are different. We could even ask students to explain their thinking. However, most students will cite the same evidence in the text and give the same basic trait a different name.

What if we followed our initial trait question with this query: *How might Anna's and Caleb's cautiousness make a difference when Sarah arrives?* This is the stuff of an interesting conversation, and suddenly your classroom is alive with ideas: *I bet Anna and Caleb will behave really well so that Sarah likes them. Maybe they'll pretend they don't like Sarah, so their feelings won't be hurt if she doesn't like them.* When you ask the right question, rigor happens!

Where will we get these great questions? Some will be specific to an individual text, and you will need to invent them on your own. But others might be more generic. It's a matter of extending the standards-based DOK 2 question. The questions shown in Figure 3.3, Extending Questions from DOK 2 to DOK 3, for Standards 1 through 8, demonstrate this. You will note that the left-hand column includes many of the same questions for Depth of Knowledge 2 from the previous chapter (see Figure 2.2). Now, a companion DOK 3 question is suggested alongside it in the right-hand column.

For Standard 9, there were no DOK 2 questions, so that standard is not represented. (Use the list of DOK 3 questions from earlier in this chapter.) For Writing, the difference between DOK 2 and DOK 3 is that Depth of Knowledge 2 expects students to *recognize* good writing, whereas Depth of Knowledge 3 challenges students to *produce* good writing. Review the list of DOK 3 Writing items earlier in this chapter for these DOK 3 expectations.

Some questions may not necessarily appear on standards-based assessments. But close reading rigor in our classroom should be driven by more than test-taking expectations.

> **Bottom Line for Aligning Rigor and Close Reading for DOK 3:** Without close reading, it is unlikely that students will ever achieve the rigor of Depth of Knowledge 3. It is this kind of deep thinking that asks students to seek meaning beyond the evidence itself: When you probe beneath the surface, what insights are revealed? What nuances of meaning can you tease from between the lines of a text? Although this might seem a tall order for teachers, it's often a matter of asking the "next" question, the one that builds on a DOK 2 response.

FIGURE 3.3 | Extending Questions from DOK 2 to DOK 3

Standard 1	
DOK 2	**DOK 3**
· Which [two] details support the conclusion _____?	· Which details are the most surprising? · Which details are the most important?

Standard 2	
DOK 2	**DOK 3**
· What is the meaning of the quote ["_____"]? Explain it in your own words. · Which sentence in the passage best describes the lesson? · Choose a sentence that best summarizes the central idea [or main idea]. Which statements belong in a summary of _____, and which statements should be left out?	· How would you explain this quote to a younger child? · How would you explain this quote to someone who didn't know anything about [Martin Luther King]? · Why did you choose this line? · What is the life lesson we can learn from this story (or significance of this information)?

Standard 3	
DOK 2	**DOK 3**
· Which words below *best* describe [Character A]? · Which word describes how _____ was <u>feeling</u>? · Where does the setting change? · What is the main problem in the story? · Arrange the events from the passage in order. · How are these events *related to* each other?	· How might [character's trait] make a difference to what happens next in the story? · What <u>motivated</u> Isabel to stand up to Greta when Greta bullied Trevor? · How did Marcus demonstrate his negative <u>attitude</u> toward his new school? · How do the characters' actions show their relationship in the story? · How might the story be different if told from _____'s <u>point of view</u>? · In what ways is the [problem] in this story *related* to the [setting]? · In your opinion, what is the turning point in this [situation/story]? Explain your thinking using details from the text. (Cannot be an obvious turning point.)

Standard 4	
DOK 2	**DOK 3**
Any DOK 2 question about context clues could be extended to focus on word choice (DOK 3).	· What effect does the author create by using the phrase _____? · What does the phrase _____ tell you about [character/problem]?

(continued)

FIGURE 3.3 | (continued)

Standard 4—(continued)	
	· What [other word/phrase] could the author have used to create the same tone? · What [word/phrase] could the author have used to create a different tone?

Standard 5	
DOK 2	**DOK 3**
· Which text feature tells about the photo? Or, How is this information provided in the article? (captions, key words, sidebar, glossary) · What is the overall structure of most paragraphs in the article? · What kind of information is the author giving us in this part of the [article]? · What craft is the author using in this part of the text?	· What is the most likely reason the author included a [map of] _____? · How does this [text feature] add to your understanding of _____? · Why do you think the author included some narrative scenes within this [cause-effect] structure? · What is the most likely reason the author wrote this piece as [a poem]? · Why did the author begin the passage with this paragraph? (Let the reader know about the problem, introduce characters, give us the message, etc.) · Why did the author choose to end this text with a [summary]? How does [paragraph 2] contribute to the development of the plot? · Why is including [dialogue] important to understanding the passage? · How does the use of [flashback] affect the events in the text? · What effect does the [quote] have on the reader's understanding? · How could you use this craft within your own writing?

Standard 6	
DOK 2	**DOK 3**
· What is the character's point of view about _____? (This could be identified as a DOK 3 question because of the inference involved. However, it is more basic than the "next step" questions for DOK 3.)	· How would this story be different if it were written from [character's] point of view? · How did the author make this poem entertaining? (Or make the article convincing, etc.) · What does the phrase [_____] suggest about the author's feelings about _____? · Why did the author write the article? · What is the difference in focus between [Source 1] and [Source 2]? · How does the author develop the narrator's point of view?

FIGURE 3.3 | (*continued*)

Standard 7	
DOK 2	**DOK 3**
· What part of the [story/article] does this [photograph] show?	· How does the [chart] add to your understanding of _____? · Why is using a [timeline] important to understanding the information in the passage? · What additional graphic would you have added to this [article] to add to meaning?
Standard 8 (Informational text only)	
DOK 2	**DOK 3**
· What kind of evidence does the author provide to support the point that _____? (interviews, statistics, opinions, experiences) · What reason does the author provide to support the point that _____? · How does the author support the claim that _____?	· Which details from the text are irrelevant to the author's claim? · Which details from the text offer the strongest support? · What could have been explained more clearly? · Which statement from the report is *not* fully supported? · What additional evidence could the author have included to make his argument more convincing? · What do you think is the most *convincing* (or *best*) evidence in support of the author's claim? Why? · Does anything in this [article] show bias? Explain.

Aligning Rigor and Student Interaction for DOK 3

Although Depth of Knowledge 3 will often culminate in students constructing written responses to questions such as those identified in Figure 3.3, conversation will be a nonnegotiable initial step if we hope to see real rigor. Conversation is where students will "draft" and "revise" their ideas before "publishing" them on paper, trying them out with the guidance of their teacher and the (hopefully) gentle critiquing of their peers.

We've all seen classroom charts of discussion etiquette—how to build on another student's response, disagree respectfully, listen politely, and the like. I trust your resourcefulness to locate one of these lists via the Internet or elsewhere if you don't already have one hanging in your classroom. But two points regarding discussion protocols will be particularly important to the rigor of DOK 3: engaging reluctant participators and listening to hear.

Engaging Reluctant Participators

No matter how supportive the classroom environment is, some students are reluctant participators. They may not enjoy engaging in discussions with their peers because they are shy or self-conscious, or quiet by nature. It's doubtful we'll turn that introvert into the life of the party. But we do need to hear that student's thinking if we're going to guide logical reasoning forward. Sometimes I solve this problem with poker chips (or any kind of marker.) Everyone gets three chips—or a different number, if you prefer. The discussion isn't over until everyone has "used up" their chips, which go into the center of the reading table when a student shares a thought that he or she has initiated.

Although I don't love strategies like this, which feel more like gimmicks than authentic teaching practices, sometimes the end justifies the means. I find that using chips in this way gets students to insert themselves into a conversation all by themselves when they may otherwise remain silent. Even if what they express is not the most profound thought, it's a starting point, and I can massage it from there. Here's an exchange with Max, a 1st grader, who seldom spoke without prompting:

> *Max* (responding to a question about Molly Lou from the book *Stand Tall, Molly Lou Melon*, by Patty Lovell): I think Molly Lou was really brave to stand up to Ronald Durkin when he bullied her, when he called her "Shrimp-o."
>
> *Me* (pushing for some logical reasoning): Excellent answer. How do you think Molly Lou got to be so brave?
>
> *Max:* She got brave because her grandma kept telling her if she acts big and strong, people won't put her down. She did what her grandma said.

Max cashed in his chip with an accurate but basic response about Molly Lou's behavior. However, it opened the door just enough so that I could ask the next, deeper question. For a 1st grader, I was satisfied with the inference about Grandma.

This chip-depositing system has some collateral benefits as well. Everyone gets the same number of chips, so the kids who would like to answer *every* question and monopolize the conversation are now restricted. They need to be selective, tossing in their chips only when they have something truly valuable to say.

Listening to Hear

There's another issue, too, that has as much to do with listening as it does with speaking. Students need to do more than listen politely and patiently; they need to listen to hear. I've watched it happen time after time, and my experience in this 5th grade classroom was a perfect example. Several students in this group had their hands in the air, eager to share their thinking about the story

"Spaghetti" from Cynthia Rylant's book *Every Living Thing*. This slim volume, perfect for intermediate-grade readers, features 12 short stories in which animals play a central and positive role. This is one of my most beloved resources, and multiple copies have accompanied me over the years to classrooms from coast to coast.

This particular tale is about a young boy named Gabriel, who, for reasons unclear to the reader, appears to be alone in the world and without any sense of purpose. He then finds a kitten (which he names Spaghetti), and that changes everything. My question, which built on another, more rudimentary one, was this: "Why do you think the author uses the color *gray* so much?"

Hands go into the air right away. I call on Jake, and the gist of his answer is that gray is a sad color. Gabriel was sad, so this color matches his mood. Jake finishes, and the same hands shoot up again, hoping for their turn. Emma takes the floor, and you think at first she is building on Jake's answer because she mentions *gray*, and how the night can appear gray, and gray is a common cat color. But in truth, this is what she was going to say all along. She simply waited (politely) until her classmate was done talking and then made her own point.

No one's reasoning will improve via polite waiting. Teach your students to make a specific link—to find a connection between their idea and the previous student's idea, or to explain how their interpretation is different. If Emma had really built on Jake's thinking, she might have said something like this: "Sometimes gray seems sad because it is almost no color at all. Before Gabriel found Spaghetti, his life seemed gray and colorless, like it had no meaning."

Model for your students what connecting to a previous comment looks like. Ask them how their response shows such a connection. Doing so will also demand more wait time between student responses. It takes time for readers to think through a genuine connection. When they race to answer, it might signal that what you will hear is their unedited opinion, not the thoughtful words that reflect consideration of a previous reply.

Bottom Line for Aligning Rigor and Student Interaction for DOK 3: Talking to each other is essential for students to build the habits of mind that lead to deep thinking. But not all talk will achieve this goal. Teachers need to recognize the point a student is making and push for the next level of reasoning. Students all need to participate so that their teacher and their peers can benefit from their thinking, and listening to *hear* is as important as engaging in the conversation themselves.

Aligning Rigor and the Reading-Writing Connection for DOK 3

Writing to sources at Depth of Knowledge 3 requires lots of rigor! This is the first DOK on new assessments for which students will probably need to construct a written response to a question. Likewise, they may also have to produce short responses that demonstrate their capacity to craft portions of a text themselves. Because analytic writing—written response to a reading question—will be such a big player on assessments, it will be addressed in the next section about aligning rigor and formative assessment. Keep reading here, though, for an instructional practice linking the writing standards to the reading standards through a narrative task.

The previous chapter laid out crafts under each writing trait so that students could identify them for the rigor of Depth of Knowledge 2. Now, for DOK 3, we need to teach students to use these crafts in their own writing. Addressing them all would require an entire book—way beyond what is reasonable in a single chapter. Instead, I will describe one high-impact strategy that can make a difference when the item states, "Revise [this paragraph] to add narrative elements like description and dialogue"—a likely expectation for students at all grade levels. This calls for the development of ideas, the first of the six writing traits.

Narrative: Making a Scene

As teachers, we explain to our students that good writing is *showing*, not *telling*, but then *we* sometimes have a hard time *showing* what we mean by this. How can we demonstrate to students how they can transform their narratives from flat and lifeless to robust and lively? Teach your students to make a scene.

This is easier than you think, armed with the four crafts that are the cornerstone of any author's narrative-writing toolbox. Provide a little *description* (which I sometimes call a "snapshot"). Include a bit of *dialogue* that builds character. Add *internal thoughts* ("thoughtshots") in which the character or narrator shares thoughts in his head with the reader that are not revealed to other characters. And don't forget *gestures* (small actions) that convey attitude.

To demonstrate to students how powerful this technique can be, give them a "stripped down" passage from a piece of children's literature. I take a short segment from a story and remove all the fun, interesting language; then ask students to rewrite it with description, dialogue, internal thoughts, and gestures. Here's a sample stripped passage:

> Sara had been looking forward to this day for a long time. She was going to audition for her school play, *Annie*. She wanted to play Annie, herself. She got out of bed and looked in her closet. She decided to wear her red sweater because the real Annie wore red. She glanced in the mirror to make sure she looked good. Her mother called her down to breakfast, but she was so excited she wasn't very hungry.

A few hours later, Sara sat on a bench outside Ms. Bartlett's door. Ms. Bartlett was the music teacher, and she was playing piano for the children as they sang their audition song. Sara noticed that she wasn't the only kid who thought to wear something red. She looked around at the other students who were auditioning for the lead role. She didn't think Rebecca would get the part because she was too quiet.

Now here's one 6th grader's version, including the four crafts:

Sara could hardly wait! This was going to be the best day of her life, the day she'd finally get to audition for the school play, *Annie*. As a 4th grader, she figured she had a chance at a big part. In fact, she wanted to play the leading role—Annie!

I just know I'll get picked to be Annie, Sara thought as she drifted off to sleep the night before. *I'm a natural actress. I even have red, curly hair like the real Annie.* She sleepily hummed a few bars to herself, *Tomorrow, tomorrow, I love ya tomorrow…*

Audition day dawned bright and sunny. Sara bounded out of bed and rustled through the clothes hanging in her closet. What could she wear that would make her really look like Annie? *I know*, she decided, *I'll wear my red sweater. Red is the color of the dress Annie always wore.* She buttoned it up so that only the top of her white turtleneck was sticking out. She glanced in the mirror, and smiled.

"Sara! Breakfast!" her mom called from the kitchen. But Sara only picked at her Cheerios. She was too excited to eat.

A few hours later, Sara sat on a bench outside Ms. Bartlett's door. Ms. Bartlett was the music teacher and she was playing piano for the children as they sang their audition song. Sara noticed that she wasn't the only kid who thought to wear red. She looked around at the other students who were auditioning. She thought to herself, *I doubt Rebecca will get to be Annie. She has such a quiet voice you can hardly hear her when she talks in class.*

Yes, this revision came from a 6th grader, and we may not receive such polished writing from a younger student. But you will be amazed by how dramatically these four crafts enhance narrative performance—immediately. This example illustrates the outcome we are seeking for DOK 3 narrative tasks such as this, and our means of getting there.

And there are a couple of bonuses. When I return to the original passage—the one before I had removed all the "good stuff"—and share it with students, they are quick to point out, "I like Martin's better." Or, "The real author didn't think to include any dialogue." Suddenly, the mystery of how authors make their writing engaging is no longer quite as mysterious. And if students can write one scene, they can write many—which is what a story is: lots of scenes strung together.

This strategy is a big win for connecting reading and writing and achieving the rigor of Depth of Knowledge 3. If you think this is a slam-dunk, check out the even higher-stakes strategy for analytic writing later in this chapter, in the section Teaching Written Response.

> **Bottom Line for Aligning Rigor and Reading-Writing Connections for DOK 3:** It is at this Depth of Knowledge that students need to put their knowledge of authors' crafts into practice. For informational and opinion/argument writing, much of the DOK focus will be on the organization of a portion of an essay or the relevance and logical connection between facts and details. For narrative writing, the strength of DOK 3 performance will be determined by competence with narrative elements.

Aligning Rigor and Formative Assessment for DOK 3

Remember that Depth of Knowledge 3 is the first DOK where learning will at times be measured through constructed response. And strange as it sounds, there will be one question that dominates: Draw a conclusion about _____, or Make an inference about _____. Often this conclusion or inference will relate to the theme or main idea. But it could also focus on point of view, the setting, the structure, or just about any dimension of a text.

Suppose the question asks this: *What inference can be made about the author's message in this passage?* This question, aligned to Standard 2 (development of a theme), relates to the excerpt from *Black Beauty* (p. 132) and the DOK 3 lesson provided on page 141 in Chapter 5. We would be happy if we got the following answer from a 5th grader who participated in this lesson:

> My inference about the author's message is that we shouldn't mistreat animals. Take Ginger, Beauty's friend. She told Beauty she had never been treated nicely from the time she was born. "I was taken from my mother as soon as I was weaned, and put with a lot of other young colts; none of them cared for me." No one ever talked to her kindly, or brought her good food to eat. Boys would throw rocks at her and they thought it was funny. Men also "wrenched her mouth open" to put on her halter. Then she was shut up in a stall all day. She wanted to get free. "You know yourself it's bad enough when you have a kind master."

If you look closely at this response, you will see it is consistent with the expectations for Standard 2 at the grade 5 level:

> Determine a theme of a story, drama, or poem from details in the text, including how characters in a story or drama respond to challenges or how the speaker in a poem reflects upon a topic; summarize the text. (http://www.corestandards.org/ELA-Literacy/RL/5/#CCSS.ELA-Literacy.RL.5.2)

The student *infers* the theme and then *summarizes* the text. This would be a full-score response based on some rubrics, whether full score is based on a 4-point scale, a 2-point scale, or something else. But some other assessments want more, including Smarter Balanced Assessment Consortium (SBAC) [see http://www.smarterbalanced.org/assessments/practice-and-training-tests/resources-and-documentation/ and click the ELA Scoring Guide for any grade level]. The SBAC criteria for a constructed response to this question is worth a total of 2 points:

A 2-point response:

- Gives sufficient evidence of the ability to make a clear inference/conclusion
- Includes specific examples/details that make clear reference to the text
- Adequately explains inference/conclusion with clearly relevant information based on the text

The third bullet point asks for an explanation or extension of the inference. To receive a full score for an answer to this question, the student would need to add a concluding thought such as this:

> These details are important because they show that animals have feelings, too. Just like Ginger, if we want animals to behave well, we should treat them the way we want to be treated.

This final component doesn't need to be long, just a sentence or two, but it does need to show the significance of the issue at hand and connect it back to the text. Regardless of whether students are scored for this final component of an inference, I like the idea of pushing for this level of reasoning. It shows an understanding of the application of a big idea to real life, beyond the boundaries of the text.

Failing to meet this criterion, or *any* criteria, will result in only partial credit:

A 1-point response:

- Gives limited evidence of the ability to make an inference/conclusion
- Includes vague/limited examples/details that make reference to the text
- Explains inference/conclusion with vague/limited information based on the text

Here's an example of a 1-point response:

> You should always be kind. Like people were kind to Beauty, but they were never kind to Ginger. She had a bad life where people hurt her and laughed at her. You should be kind, not mean like it shows in this story.

A no-credit response, according to SBAC, has the following flaws:

A 0-point response:

- Gives no evidence of the ability to make an inference/conclusion

OR

- Gives an inference/conclusion but includes no examples or examples/ details that make reference to the text

OR

- Gives an inference/conclusion but includes no explanation or no relevant information from the text

Consider the following example:

Some horses have bad behavior. Ginger wanted to run away.

Now, what do we need to do to teach students to produce high-quality written responses?

Teaching Written Response

Plain and simple, students need to know that responding in writing to an inference question is a three-step process, and it's the same sequence whether the text is literary or informational:

1. Answer the question (the inference/conclusion/main idea).
2. Summarize the main points in the story/article.
3. Extend/explain.

If you've addressed the matter of oral rehearsal (explained in the previous chapter), that instruction will benefit students here. But there are additional guidelines that will support students as well.

If students are stuck on the first step of this process, making an inference about theme or some other textual component, that is a reading problem, not a writing problem. Identifying a theme or main idea can be difficult, and backtracking to DOK 2, where this skill is taught, is your best option. If students can't determine the theme or main idea, there's no way they can move forward with the rest of their response.

The second step of the response should be manageable because it asks only for evidence—literal knowledge of the text. The difficulty here is that the rubric for a 2-point response is misleading: *includes specific examples/details that make clear reference to the text*. This leads teachers and students to believe that an example or two will get the job done. It will not—despite how we may have taught this in the past. Recall the last phrase in the grade 5 benchmark for Standard 2 (p. 92–93): *summarize the text*. The same expectation prevails for all grade levels and is also represented in the anchor standard. Students need to show how the author *develops* the theme or main idea. There are no shortcuts here, and what is needed for successful completion of this part of the response is sufficient stamina as well as adequate comprehension.

"You've got this. Keep going," I prodded a 5th grader whose energy for the task appeared to be waning. When I introduce written response, I do it in small groups where I can keep a close eye on students' progress. In its early stages, written response is more instruction than assessment.

This nurturing is even more important for the third and final part of the answer, the extension or explanation. Even when students persevere through the citing of evidence, I've seen a few come to a screeching halt when they reach this step. One forthright young lady put down her pencil and looked up at me imploringly: "I have absolutely no idea what to write here." Many students will feel the same way if we are not proactive in helping them understand what this part of the response is asking of them.

What we're really asking is this: *What is the life lesson? Why is this important?* And the irony (in this era where *everything* is evidence-based) is that no amount of going back to the text will resolve this. This thinking comes from insights derived partly from reading and partly from background knowledge built outside school, or in school through discussion of topics in history, social studies, and science. *Why* is it important to protect endangered animals? *How* do we show integrity? *What* qualities make a great leader? Can we extend our disciplinary teaching to ponder these "what ifs"? Or, more fundamentally, "what if" we're not teaching enough history or science content to even have these conversations?

Helping Students Achieve Deeper Insights by Asking "What If"

Begin by revisiting the theme chart in Figure 2.3 and discussing some of these big ideas alongside contrasting perspectives: *When is courage important? When is it best not to take a chance? If cooperation is the goal, is it ever acceptable to take control?* If students can talk about these "life connections," they will be more likely to succeed on this part of their written response.

Having the language to get started on this part of the answer helps, too. See the chart Guidelines for Explaining and Extending Your Answer (Figure 7.3) in Chapter 7, page 161, for words and phrases to initiate an explanation.

Guiding students through the three steps of a quality written response to an inference question may be easier if they have a visual reference to keep them on track. See Figure 7.4, Stepping Up to Success: Answering a Question to Draw a Conclusion or Make an Inference, in Chapter 7, page 162. For easy reference, place this graphic on your small-group-instruction table or provide a copy to each student for safe keeping in their reading folder.

There has been a lot to digest in this chapter, which is not surprising, as there is so much rigor expected for Depth of Knowledge 3. Now it's time to move on to Chapter 4 and the even deeper thinking required of Depth of Knowledge 4.

Bottom Line for Aligning Rigor and Formative Assessment for DOK 3: When assessing DOK 3, be sure to provide opportunities for written response and look beyond inference to insight. Can students use textual evidence to draw a conclusion or make an inference? Can they support their inference or conclusion with relevant text-based details? And then can they recognize a broader context for an idea, linking it to a life lesson or real-world implication?

4

Extended Thinking: Supporting Depth of Knowledge 4

This is where all roads meet, where everything we've been teaching students about literacy through Depths of Knowledge 1 through 3 comes together. It's hard to tell that, however, from the brief definition in Figure 4.1: *Using extended thinking*. This definition implies that we will expect DOK 4 tasks to require more time for students to complete. But that should not be its only distinguishing characteristic.

FIGURE 4.1 | Depth of Knowledge 4 and Rigor

Depth of Knowledge 4	The Rigor
Using extended thinking	Creativity in synthesizing information, often from multiple sources or points of view

Underlying Principles: Rigor for DOK 4

Think about *why* DOK 4 tasks may require more time—the rigor involved. Students will need more time for DOK 4 tasks because there will often be more reading involved—two sources, and possibly three or more. Then there's the time needed for processing multiple texts: How do they connect? How can the content from all sources be integrated? And finally, what kind of product can be created that reflects each student's individuality? A worthy DOK 4 task should afford the potential for not only critical thinking but also creative thinking. For this, we need a better understanding of the rigor involved in creative thinking.

A good general definition of creative thinking might be this one, from the online *Business Dictionary*: "a way of looking at problems or situations from a fresh perspective that suggests unorthodox solutions (which might look unsettling at first)" (http://www.businessdictionary.com/definition/creative-thinking .html). This out-of-the-box thinking has four distinguishing criteria: flexibility, fluency, originality, and elaboration (Henkel, 2002).

Applied to a literacy task, the four criteria might look like this:

- *Flexibility*—In the planning process, the student examines many possibilities and approaches before moving forward with an idea.
- *Fluency*—The thinking includes *many* details, ideas, or examples—more than would be expected.
- *Originality*—The perspective is plausible but truly unique, clever, and unusual, a new way of looking at a situation or problem.
- *Elaboration*—The thinking is well developed, with thorough expansion of each idea, maximizing clarity through carefully articulated details.

What kinds of tasks lend themselves to the rigor of creative thinking? Let's look at what new standards-based assessments are asking students to do to demonstrate their capacity to synthesize information from multiple sources or points of view.

Measuring DOK 4 on Standards-Based Assessments

DOK 4 items almost always involve both reading and writing and are frequently regarded as performance-based tasks. They may differ considerably from state to state. When states move away from the two consortium-based Common Core assessments—the tests designed by the Smarter Balanced Assessment Consortium (SBAC) and the Partnership for the Assessment of Readiness for College and Career (PARCC)—they find that this is the part of the test that changes the most. The standards-based questions for reading remain about the same on all assessments, but there can be wide variation on measures of writing, as well as the amount of writing students are asked to do.

Performance tasks are typically a collection of questions. Some of these questions measure reading, often using multiple-choice items that tap students' understanding of the way sources connect to each other. A few questions call for a constructed response. The reading-related questions are generally aligned with DOK 3, although a limited number that call for students to write about their reading are considered DOK 4. An example of a DOK 4 short-answer item is this: *Which source would most likely be the most helpful in locating information about _____?*

The second component of the performance task, the feature that calls for the most "extended thinking," is sometimes referred to as the "full write." Here, students are tasked with writing a full essay or story. These are generally untimed but ask for several pages, or the equivalent of several pages if the test is taken online. Issues surrounding technology, such as young children's lack of keyboarding skills and difficulty navigating the screen layout of a test's content, elicit cries of deep concern from teachers everywhere. I feel your pain, but I can't fix it. We need to stay on track here for instructional priorities where our efforts can make a difference. Increased knowledge of the kinds of full-write items students will probably see on new assessments can lead them in the right direction while also helping them to become better writers.

The full-write tasks identified here are similar to items I've retrieved from various assessments. I've changed the exact content of the questions, but the format is the same. All measures involve writing to sources—often two or more. The tasks fall into several categories: narrative, literary analysis, opinion/argument, informative/explanatory, and research.

Examples of Narrative Tasks

1. Your task is to write a story about the United States in the 1840s. You will write your story from the point of view of a 10-year-old child traveling west with his family to Oregon. Your story will be read by parents, teachers, and other students in your school. You should use information from the two articles you read about traveling to the West in a covered wagon to write your story. In your story, describe why your family decided to leave your home in the East, what your journey was like, and the challenges you faced along the way. When writing your story, find ways to use information and details from the sources to improve your story. Make sure you develop your character(s), the setting, and the plot, using details, dialogue, and description.

2. You have read two fables and an article about fables. Write an original fable of your own using features of a fable explained in the article. Use the two fables you read as models for how to develop your story. Be sure to include narrative elements such as details, dialogue, and description.

3. This story tells about Melanie's audition for the school play, *Annie*. As the story ends, you still don't know whether Melanie was chosen to play the part of Annie, the role she wanted so badly. You *do* know that she was worried that her audition had not gone well. Write Melanie's journal entry about her audition after the audition was over, including her feelings about being in the play. Include information related to the events in the story as you write the journal entry. Be sure to include narrative elements such as details, dialogue, and description.

4. In the story you read, "A Fright for Alex," a boy gets lost in the woods and experiences scary moments before his family finds him. Think about

the details the author uses to create the characters, settings, and events. Imagine that you, like the boy in the story, get lost in the woods while on a hike with your family. Write a story about your scary moments and how you finally solve your problem. Use what you have learned about getting lost in the woods when writing your story. Be sure to include narrative elements such as details, dialogue, and description.

5. You have read a passage from *Cinderella* in which the story is told from Cinderella's point of view. In this passage, she is complaining about her mean stepsisters and all the work they are making her do. Think about how the story would be different if it were told from one of the stepsisters' point of view. Rewrite this story from the point of view of one of the stepsisters. Be sure to include narrative elements such as details, dialogue, and description.

6. In the passage from *Sara Crewe*, the author creates a problem and two distinct characters—Sara and her new friend, Ermengarde. Think about the details the author uses to establish the problem and the characters. Write an original story about what happens when Sara reads the books given to her by Ermengarde and they meet to discuss them. In your story, be sure to use what you have learned about the problem and the characters as you tell what happens next. Be sure to include narrative elements such as details, dialogue, and description.

Examples of Literary Analysis Tasks

1. Based on this chapter from *The Adventures of Tom Sawyer* about whitewashing the fence, write an essay to explain how the author shows that Tom Sawyer was a clever person. Be sure to use information from the passage to develop your essay.

2. Look at the illustrations from both fables. How does each one help you to understand the problem in the story more clearly? Be sure to use evidence from both fables to support your answer.

3. Based on the journal entry and the poem, write an essay to explain how prejudice can affect people. Be sure to use information from both the journal entry and the poem to develop your essay.

4. Write an essay explaining how the themes in the excerpt from *Old Yeller* by Fred Gipson and the excerpt from *Shiloh* by Phyllis Reynolds Naylor are similar. Be sure to use details from both passages to develop your essay.

5. Both [Source 1] and [Source 2] are set in a region with a very cold climate. Write an essay that compares how each source uses the cold climate in a different way. Be sure to use important details from both texts. Organize your essay to compare the setting.

6. Compare the author's point of view in the poem "I Hear America Singing" by Walt Whitman to the point of view in the poem "I, Too, Sing America" by Langston Hughes. Be sure to use details from both poems to develop your essay.

7. Abraham Lincoln's character is revealed in the poem "Abraham Lincoln" by Berton Bellis and also in the excerpt you read from the lecture "Abraham Lincoln" by Henry Watterson. Write an essay that explains how both the poem and the lecture excerpt help you understand the character of Abraham Lincoln. Be sure to use information from both sources to develop your essay. (I have also seen this question for younger readers, asking for two character traits and how these traits affect the plot.)

Examples of Opinion/Argument Tasks

1. Your class has been discussing the advantages and disadvantages of a longer school day because this is something your city is considering. Your classmates have different opinions about this issue. Your teacher has asked all students in your class to write a letter to the editor stating your opinion about a longer school day. He will send the best two letters, pro and con, to the newspaper to be published.

   Your assignment is to use the information from the three articles you read to write an opinion paper about a longer school day. Make sure you clearly state your opinion and write several paragraphs supporting your opinion with reasons for or against a longer day, using details from the sources. Develop your ideas clearly and use your own words, except when quoting directly from the sources. Be sure to give the source title or number for the details or facts you use.

2. When your class returns from the zoo, your classmates begin to share what they learned about different kinds of zoo animals. They also begin to discuss whether animals should be confined to zoos. Some students are not in favor of zoos, while others think zoos are acceptable. Your teacher asks you to write a paper presenting an argument for or against zoos.

   In your paper, you will take a side as to whether you think zoos are acceptable or not acceptable. Your paper will be read by your teacher and your classmates. Make sure you clearly state your claim and write several paragraphs supporting the claim with reasons based on information in the two articles provided to you about zoos. Be sure to refute possible claims from the opposing viewpoint. Develop your ideas clearly and use your own words, except when quoting directly from the sources. Be sure to give the source title or number for the details or facts you use.

Examples of Informative/Explanatory Tasks

1. Your class is creating a website about the importance of clean drinking water for everyone in the world. Your task is to write an informational article about the problems that occur when drinking water is *not* clean, places in the world where getting clean water is a challenge, and possible solutions to this problem. Your article will be read by other students, teachers, and parents.

   Using all three of the sources provided to you, develop a main idea about the importance of clean drinking water. Choose the most important information from each source to support your main idea. Then, write an informational article about your main idea that is several paragraphs long. Clearly organize your article and support your main idea with details from the sources. Use your own words except when quoting directly from the sources.

2. Now that you have completed research on the topic of wind farms for your science club, your club advisor has asked you to write an explanatory article about wind farms for the next issue of the school newspaper. The audience for your article will be other students, teachers, and parents.

   Using more than one source, develop a thesis about the value of wind farms. Once you have determined your thesis, select the most relevant information from more than one source to support this idea. Then write a multiparagraph article explaining your thesis. Clearly organize your article and elaborate your ideas. Unless quoting directly from the sources, use your own words. Be sure to reference the source title or number when quoting or paraphrasing details or facts from the sources.

Examples of Research Tasks

1. Your friend thinks it would be impossible for people to make their home in a desert. Write a letter to your friend based on information from the articles "How Do People Live in the Desert?" and "How People Live in the Sahara Desert." Use ideas and facts from both articles in your letter to show that people can live in a desert.

2. You have read two texts about scientists doing research in Antarctica. Both provide information about the climate, the plants and animals that live there, and the effect that scientists' research is having on this land of ice and snow. Think about each author's point of view on this topic. Write an essay that compares the viewpoint of both authors. Remember to use text evidence to support your ideas.

Aligning Rigor and Standards for DOK 4

As noted in the opening sentence of this chapter, DOK 4 is where all roads meet, where *all* standards come together. In fact, there are so many standards in play simultaneously at this Depth of Knowledge that it is often hard to recognize them individually. Because students need to write to sources, there are always reading standards involved—related to theme or point of view or some other aspect of comprehension.

Because students are often expected to read multiple sources before responding in writing, DOK 4 focuses on Common Core Reading Standard 9, which emphasizes connections between texts. We will examine the rigor of text connections later in this chapter in the section Aligning Rigor and Close Reading for Depth of Knowledge 4. We'll examine alignment to the writing standards here.

Standards Emphasized for DOK 4

Just like the Common Core standards for Reading, the first three Writing standards address "what"—*what* are students writing? Is the goal to present an opinion or argument (Standard 1)? Is it to explain or inform (Standard 2)? Or is it to tell a story (Standard 3)? For SBAC measures or assessments based on SBAC, the link to these standards is easy to spot because the task is labeled "Opinion/Argument," "Explanatory/Informative," or "Narrative."

Full-write tasks, called "Prose Constructed Responses" on PARCC assessments or PARCC-based assessments, are not as clear cut. There is a "Narrative" requirement, calling for a story. But then there are tasks for "Literary Analysis" and "Research." These incorporate elements of both informative/explanatory writing and opinion/argument writing. Although they are not as specifically aligned to the actual standards, they are most definitely aligned to the types of writing expected of students as they progress through elementary, middle, and high school—in preparation for the writing they will be expected to do in college. Students do lots of research, and analyzing literature is a staple of most middle and high school language arts and English programs.

Unfortunately, students could be knowledgeable about all types of writing and still fall short on a writing assessment. Why? There are other Writing standards that also affect writing competence. Writing Standard 4 focuses on the development, organization, and style of a piece of writing, which I regard as craft. Authors' craft was discussed in the previous chapter for DOK 3 Writing expectations. Again, if we spent more time addressing the elements of craft in the kinds of "brief writes" expected for DOK 3, students would have a more solid writing foundation to bring to DOK 4.

We can say the same for Writing Standard 5, centered on the *process* of writing—planning, drafting, revising, editing, and rewriting. Students will need to fine-tune these skills throughout their entire academic career—in fact, their entire lives. But getting started before encountering the rigorous mandates of DOK 4 will reduce the anxiety of putting so many writing expectations in place at one time. Let's proceed by taking a deeper look at the challenges of what's new in writing for Depth of Knowledge 4—writing lengthy pieces for all types of writing.

The Format of DOK 4 Items

One thing you may notice right away about the format of DOK 4 items is their length—as in *long*. Students often need to wade through many sentences and sometimes multiple paragraphs to discover what the item is asking them to do. We need to teach students to analyze a writing task step by step to tease out all the specifications. Here's an example based on the argument task about zoos presented earlier:

> When your class returns from the zoo, your classmates begin to share what they learned about different kinds of zoo animals. They also begin to discuss whether animals should be confined to zoos. Some students are not in favor of zoos, while others think zoos are acceptable.

This part of the item provides a context. It makes the task more authentic to students because they can see themselves as part of this scenario.

The next part of the item is straightforward:

> Your teacher asks you to write a paper presenting an argument for or against zoos.

By the end of this paragraph, students know what their writing task will be (argument), though not yet the details of the assignment. Above all, make sure students are vigilant about looking for the type of writing they will be expected to do.

The item continues:

> In your paper, you will take a side as to whether you think zoos are acceptable or not acceptable.

Here it is: the exact task. Students need to choose one of these options. All DOK 4 writing charges are laid out with precision. Part of the challenge for students is sticking to the topic!

The item goes on to provide additional information:

> Your paper will be read by your teacher and your classmates.

Now students have a sense of audience. If their paper is to be read by their teacher and their classmates, what tone and writing style would be appropriate? Although including this sentence may seem unnecessary, it again adds to the context.

Next, the item offers some specific guidance:

> Make sure you state your claim and write several paragraphs supporting
> the claim with reasons based on information in the two articles provided
> to you about zoos. Be sure to refute possible claims from the opposing
> viewpoint.

Students should note every detail of their task. Here they should recognize
that they are expected to begin with a claim and then write several paragraphs
defending it, using information they have retrieved from their sources. Yes, their
sources! Not information they've amassed from their vast fund of prior knowledge on a topic or "facts" that they invent. This is a greater challenge for younger
students who sometimes can't tell you exactly where their information came
from.

Another feature of this task is the requirement of arguing against counterclaims. Whatever requirements are spelled out, students need to take note of
them.

Here's the conclusion of the item:

> Develop your ideas clearly and use your own words, except when quoting
> directly from the sources. Be sure to give the source title or number for
> the details or facts you use.

The final task component clarifies the expectations for craft. These expectations will be similar for opinion/argument writing, informative/explanatory
writing, research, and literary analysis. The crafting expectations for narrative
will generally identify the need for "narrative elements such as details, dialogue,
and description."

A final complication for DOK 4 writing items is the way they appear in
either the online version of a test or a pencil-paper version. In an online test, students may see a relatively small box where they will type their response. *Great*,
they may think to themselves. *This is just a little box. Little boxes only need a
little writing*. But, of course, this is incorrect—the box will expand as they write.
Be sure your students are aware of this.

The reverse is true of paper-pencil writing assessments. Students as young
as 3rd graders may be given four lined pages to fill. Even as adults, many of us
would find this intimidating. Students need to know that they do not have to fill
all four pages. But they *are* expected to write more than a couple of paragraphs.

Where to Increase Instructional Focus for DOK 4

Of the three basic modes of writing—narrative, explanatory/informative,
and opinion/argument—it was opinion/argument writing that garnered the
most fanfare early on. How could young children manage this type of writing,
which was typically reserved for older students? We need not have worried, for
if there's one thing kids are good at, it's arguing. They learn to defend their opinion at an early age as they resolve conflicts with parents and siblings. Now they

need to apply this skill to sources they have read rather than experiences they have lived.

Another way of looking at this is that opinion/argument writing is essentially informative/explanatory writing with *attitude*. And informative/explanatory writing is typically a longer version of the kind of written response that students write for questions at Depth of Knowledge 3. We will examine the rigor of all three types of writing. But we'll begin with narrative, which has proven to be more complex than originally assumed.

The Challenges of Narrative Writing

The most challenging aspect of narrative writing is the many kinds of stories students can be asked to write. Each of the six narrative tasks described on pages 99–100 represents a unique complexity.

Narrative Task 1, in this case about a trip west in a covered wagon, asks students to write a story based on their understanding of *informational* sources. This is an entirely new expectation for students' narrative writing, and one that represents a significant instructional shift. "Write about what you know," we tell our students. But is this always sound advice? Think about any novel you've read recently. Chances are, the author had to do a considerable amount of research on her topic before she could write about it. Students will not thrive on a question of this kind if the first time they see it is on an assessment. Just imagine the potential, however, if we teach our students that the product they generate from informational reading through their science or social studies instruction could take the shape of a story, not just analytical writing. This is a great example of the creative thinking that can emerge from an extended-thinking task.

Narrative Task 2, in the example about writing a fable, emphasizes genre knowledge as well as using informational sources to write a story. Understanding genre elements is an area of need that begins at Depth of Knowledge 2. This task calls for writing a fable. But it could be a fairy tale, a tall tale, an adventure story, a mystery, historical fiction, fantasy, or something else. If we guided students to identify genre characteristics each time we read fiction, we would be supporting their comprehension and helping them recognize how these characteristics come together when *they* write in that genre.

Narrative Task 3 relates to writing a journal entry, which presents a few challenges. For students, the most difficult feature of this type of task is assuming the identity of the character, writing in the first person, and continuing that perspective through the entire piece. Some students slip back into third person and suddenly you're reading about what "she" did. Another issue for students is maintaining the same traits and feelings the character expressed in the story that they read. In the case of the specific prompt presented earlier, Melanie cannot express confidence and a positive outlook now, when throughout the story she was so disappointed in her performance. For teachers, the challenge of a journal task is to make it specific. Don't ask students to "write a journal entry about Melanie's audition." This will yield a laundry list of reflections from the beginning to the end of the experience. Give them a point in time: before she went to bed the night before her audition; just before the audition; after the audition. Now the journal entry can describe that small moment in depth.

Narrative Task 4, using a story as a model for writing your own story, is potentially one of the trickiest narrative assignments we could give kids. There's some value in providing students a model of good writing on a topic. But the downside is that after they've seen how the author has worked out the plot, it's hard for them to imagine a different storyline. Many times students will produce a story that is essentially the same as the one they just read. If you use this format for narrative practice, be sure to give students time to brainstorm options for their very own adventure. And choose a topic that students are likely to have some prior knowledge about.

Narrative Task 5, telling a story from an alternate point of view, is a wonderful exercise in understanding character. As in Narrative Task 3, be sure to identify a specific scene—one that includes strong indicators of a character's traits, feelings, motivations, and attitude. The best sources for this kind of task are written in the first person and have another character with a sharply contrasting point of view.

Narrative Task 6, asking what happens next, is a popular assessment task and an excellent option for instruction as well. There are two likely possibilities. Sometimes students read an entire story and are asked to write a sequel—a new story that includes the same characters, now faced with a different problem. For this writing, students need to consider what they know about the characters and whether those characters learned anything from their previous experience. The other possibility for "what happens next" writing is that students will read part of a story and be asked to complete it. This requires understanding of both the characters and the conflict. Picture books with a problem-solution structure are great resources for this. Read to the turning point—and stop! By this time students will know enough about the story elements to infer possible events leading to an outcome.

The Challenges of Literary Analysis

Whereas DOK 4 tasks for narrative writing draw heavily on what students know about the craft of writing, literary analysis is grounded in deep comprehension. PARCC-based assessments include literary analysis beginning in 3rd grade—and teachers complain mightily about this. "Do you think this is developmentally appropriate?" they implore. I remember learning the art of serious literary analysis in high school English, and even then there was a learning curve. But I suspect we would confront growing pains at whatever grade we introduced literary analysis. And although older students will be capable of thinking that is more abstract, I also believe that younger students can become good analyzers of literary texts—with the right instruction.

This begs the question: What is the "right instruction" for literary analysis? Simply put, students need more lessons in making text-to-text connections. This instruction will be addressed later in this chapter in the section Aligning Rigor and Close Reading. Here we will identify the kinds of text connections we want students to make based on the literary analysis tasks described on pages 100–101, and the challenges they imply.

Literary Analysis Task 1, which asks students to analyze the iconic "white-washing" scene from *Tom Sawyer,* is an example of a task to be completed at the 3rd or 4th grade level. Note that there are not even two sources to compare here. Students need only examine one text for examples of a character trait, and that trait is identified for them: *cleverness.* The task would require explaining what it means to be "clever" and then showing the development of this trait throughout the passage. If this sounds familiar, it's because it is identical to the constructed response required for Depth of Knowledge 3. Will younger students ever compare texts? Yes, but analyzing one text thoroughly is a worthy starting point.

Literary Analysis Task 2 asks students to focus on illustrations as keys to meaning. For this connection, choose texts with powerful images, and highlight the connection between the illustration and a specific text component like character, problem, or setting. You can also incorporate informational sources and the photographs that accompany them, but remember that technically, this is not "literary" analysis.

Literary Analysis Task 3 integrates a fictional journal entry and a poem. This task offers a good reminder to think outside the box when choosing sources for analysis—not just stories, but also poems, illustrations, art prints, scenes from plays, and more. Even music and dance could be combined with a literary source and analyzed for mood, point of view, or theme.

Literary Analysis Task 4 is aimed at comparing texts based on a common theme: How did the author of Source 1 develop this theme? How did the author of Source 2 develop the same theme? Sometimes the theme will be identified. Other times, as in this example, students must determine the theme for themselves. This is a very common assessment question and should be on your short list of important text connections to address with your students.

Literary Analysis Tasks 5–7 are similar to Task 4 but focus on other textual elements like setting, character, problem, point of view—and just about anything else that could be compared between sources. Hint: Don't be afraid to invent some unlikely comparisons, such as a fairy tale alongside a biography of a world leader, or a poem by Shel Silverstein together with a poem by Emily Dickinson. If you want to elicit a unique product from students, give them something to ponder that demands their creative thinking—truly the stuff of Depth of Knowledge 4.

The Challenges of Opinion/Argument Tasks

I identified fewer examples of opinion/argument tasks because they are all quite similar. Moreover, I deconstructed the argument task on pages 104–105, so we now have a good idea what this kind of task requires and the ways it challenges students. As with tasks for all types of writing, be alert to Common Core benchmark variations from grade to grade. I work most often with the anchor standards because I want to focus on essential principles of organization and development for each kind of writing. The benchmarks are helpful when you want to determine suitable rigor in each area for a grade level. But often I find myself asking slightly more of students if it seems reasonable.

The transition from "opinion" to "argument" is a case in point. In 5th grade, students write *opinion* pieces "on topics or texts, supporting a point of view with reasons and information." In 6th grade, they write *arguments* "to support claims with clear reasons and relevant evidence." In 7th grade, they also write *arguments*, but now "acknowledge alternate or opposing claims" (http://www.core-standards.org/ELA-Literacy/). There are other small shifts within these grades, too, but it's the difference in language between grades 5 and 6 and the addition of counterclaims in grade 7 that stand out most. I do not find the *argument* terminology ("claims" and "relevant evidence") and even the concept of "counterclaims" to be too sophisticated for 5th graders, and possibly even younger students. Although educators sometimes bemoan standards benchmarks that demand too much, the reverse can also be true. Don't let a prescribed benchmark hold your students back if you know they can aim higher.

Don't let a prescribed benchmark hold your students back if you know they can aim higher.

The Challenges of Informative/Explanatory Tasks and Research Tasks

You will note that these tasks are titled differently, but the expectations for students are about the same: read multiple informational sources and write an expository essay on the topic. There is no clear distinction between the terms *explanatory* and *informative*. However, both terms imply that the purpose is to educate on a subject, not to give an opinion or convince someone to do something.

Labeling this same kind of assignment "research" is a bit of a stretch. The outcome may be the same: an essay elaborating on a topic based on sources. But real research should also include the search itself. Providing students with the sources eliminates what is often the greatest challenge—finding the best resources to support your topic. Although it may be unrealistic to hold assessments to this standard, we can do better within our instruction. When students are doing their own research in your classroom, expect them to gather their own sources before they write.

Preparing for the Challenges of Different Types of Writing

It is likely that several types of writing will be expected of students at any grade level. This expectation means a strong district or school writing

We need to recognize that developing writing competence is a years-long journey that all teachers need to embrace.

curriculum should incorporate different types of writing every year. The guidelines provided here and elsewhere in this chapter will lead you toward instructional practices that *teach* writing instead of just *assessing* it. We need to do more than give students opportunities to *practice* their writing. We need to explain the similarities between writing modes and the peculiarities of each one. We need to show them good models of various types of writing. And then we do need them to practice—a lot. Most of all, we need to recognize that developing writing competence is a years-long journey that *all* teachers need to embrace. It is not a quick fix that can be accomplished by a few teachers here and there with the courage to take up this charge.

> **Bottom Line for Aligning Rigor and Standards for DOK 4:** This Depth of Knowledge integrates reading standards with writing standards. However, DOK 4 is measured by students' capacity to *write*. For this reason, it is imperative that we understand the challenges within each type of writing so that we can best support our students. It is equally important for our curriculum to incorporate all types of writing every year.

Aligning Rigor and Text Complexity for DOK 4

Regardless of the type of writing students are expected to do on assessments, in most states, they will be writing to sources. With so many types of writing, how will we choose? How will we align rigor and text complexity for Depth of Knowledge 4? The essence of effective instruction for Depth of Knowledge 4 is choosing texts that work well together. Without that, students can't make connections between texts as they read or write.

On standards-based assessments, the connected texts will be short because students need to get the reading done and move on to their writing. Within our literacy instruction, sources can be longer. But texts that are too long—a multichapter novel, for example—become unwieldy for assessments—even a classroom assessment. We want students to engage with novels and longer informational sources, but these may not be the best materials for elementary and middle school when you want students to make text connections.

We can, and should, vary our sources beyond the excerpts and other short pieces students typically find on an assessment. I suggest picture books, articles, and poems as places to begin. The resources listed in Chapter 6 (Books and Other Resources That Inspire Deep Thinking) and featured in Chapters 2, 3, and

4 were chosen because they can be combined into text sets around a common central idea. I have created five possible text sets for each grade range: K–2, 3–5, and 6–8.

Each text set includes three sources, often both informational and literary, though a teacher may choose to use only two of the identified texts; and, in fact, some types of writing (literary analysis, for example) typically include only two sources. Narrative items often focus on a single source. For each text set, I propose two types of writing tasks, suitable for developmentally appropriate topics of study within each grade range. Use your imagination to invent others. Also, use these sets as models to design your own text sets aligned with your grade-level curriculum.

Text Sets for Grades K–2

Central idea: Treating people fairly

- *Stand Tall, Molly Lou Mellon*
- *Amazing Grace*
- "Meet Rosa Parks" (informational article)

Explanatory: Write a paragraph that explains how each of these people or characters were treated unfairly.

Opinion: In your opinion, which of these people or characters was treated the most unfairly? Explain your thinking in a paragraph with details from the book or article.

Central idea: Solving a mystery

- "The Wind" (poem)
- "The New Kid on the Block" (poem)
- *Eggbert*

Literary Analysis: What is the author's message in the book *Eggbert*? Tell what this message is and explain in a paragraph how the author showed this message with details from the story. Include at least two details.

Narrative: Reread the poem "The New Kid on the Block." How does the author help you picture the bully in your mind? Write a paragraph that describes a bully using different details. Make sure readers can picture this bully based on the details you give.

Central idea: Finding beauty in your world

- *Something Beautiful*
- *Last Stop on Market Street*
- "World Wonders" (informational article)

Opinion: In your opinion, which is the most amazing world wonder? Use details about this wonder to write a paragraph explaining why you think it is so amazing.

Literary Analysis: The little girl in *Something Beautiful* says, "Beautiful means something that when you have it, your heart is happy." Write a paragraph with some examples from this book and *Last Stop on Market Street* that show things that made these characters' hearts happy.

Central idea: What's the harm?

- *Turtle, Turtle, Watch Out!*
- *Never Smile at a Monkey*
- "Should You Be Afraid of Sharks?" (informational article)

Explanatory/Research: Choose two animals that you read about in these sources. How can each one be harmful to you? Using details from these sources, write a paragraph explaining the danger of each animal.

Narrative: You are walking along a beach and you see a baby sea turtle. Write a story about what happens next. How can you help this turtle? Use information from *Turtle, Turtle, Watch Out!* to help protect this little turtle.

Text Sets for Grades 3–5

Central idea: Overcoming challenges/achieving dreams

- *More Than Anything Else*
- "Mother to Son" (poem)
- "A Chance for Freedom" (informational article)

Opinion: Choose at least two sources. In your opinion, which challenges described in these sources were the most difficult to overcome? Identify these challenges and explain how the main character or person overcame them. Write an essay of several paragraphs with evidence from your sources to support your thinking. Conclude with a life lesson that extends beyond the sources to the world today.

Narrative: Using the poem "Mother to Son," write a letter to a friend explaining important choices to make to lead a successful life and achieve your dreams. This poem uses the metaphor of a staircase to explain life choices. Can you think of a different metaphor to include in your letter? (Your letter does not need to be written as a poem.)

Central idea: Righting a wrong/showing character

- *The Summer My Father Was Ten*
- *The Can Man*

- "Your Name in Gold" (short story)

Literary Analysis: Life is full of choices. Sometimes we make good choices, and other times our choices are not so good. All main characters in these books made choices. Which were good choices? Which were poor choices? Choose two of these sources and compare the choices characters made. What made them good choices or poor choices?

Narrative: Reread the story "Your Name in Gold." Think about what you know about Anne and Mary and the problem they had. Write a story about another situation in which these two girls both want the same thing, but only one of them can have it. What do they want? What happens when they disagree? Did they learn anything from their experience with the pin? Think about what you know about each of these girls as you write your story.

Central idea: Only love can drive out hate

- *Martin's Big Words*
- "The Ballad of Birmingham" (poem)
- "A Tale of Segregation: Fetching Water" (informational article)

Explanatory/Research: Each of these sources describes events that really happened. Using at least two of these sources, explain how prejudice is harmful to people. Use details from your sources as evidence.

Opinion: In your opinion, what is the most important quote in *Martin's Big Words*? Choose your quote and give three reasons why it is so meaningful. Use evidence from this source and at least one of the other two sources to support your thinking. Write a conclusion that explains why this quote is important even in our world today.

Central idea: Friends in a time of need

- *Pink and Say*
- *Mercedes and the Chocolate Pilot: A True Story of the Berlin Airlift and the Candy That Dropped from the Sky*
- "Spaghetti" (short story)

Literary Analysis: A central idea in all of these stories is the importance of friendship. Write an essay that begins with your definition of what makes a great friend. Then, using evidence from two sources, show how the characters in these stories are examples of "great friends." End your essay with a life lesson about why friendship is important to people's happiness.

Narrative: Continue the story of "Spaghetti." What happens when Gabriel brings the kitten home? Is he allowed to keep it? What happens next? Maybe there will be some new characters in your story (Gabriel's parents, for example). As you write your story, think about the kind of boy Gabriel is and what is important to him. Be sure your story includes narrative crafts like description and dialogue.

Central idea: It all depends on your perspective

- Lou Gehrig's "Farewell" (speech)
- *Freedom Summer*
- *Voices in the Park*

Explanatory: Lou Gehrig made the best of a very bad situation. In fact, he thought he was the "luckiest man." Reread this speech to identify all the reasons Lou Gehrig thought he was lucky. Explain them in an essay using evidence from this source. In your final paragraph, explain why you agree or disagree with Lou Gehrig's thinking.

Narrative: Choose a specific moment in *Freedom Summer*. It could be the moment when Joe and John Henry first learn they will be able to swim together in the town pool. It could be when they arrive at the pool and discover that no one will be going for a swim. It could be another moment. Write about this moment in a journal entry as if you were John Henry. Then change your perspective and write the entry as if you were Joe. How would each of these boys see this situation differently? Be sure your journal entries include narrative elements like description and dialogue.

Text Sets for Grades 6–8

Central idea: Becoming who you are

- "Still I Rise" (poem)
- *The Three Questions*
- "Taking Down the Green-Eyed Monster" (informational article)

Literary analysis: Using two of these sources, how does each author develop the theme of becoming who you are? Show the similarities and differences using details from both sources.

Narrative: Using information from "Taking Down the Green-Eyed Monster," write a story in which a character is experiencing jealousy. Solve the problem based on suggestions in this article.

Central idea: Defining loyalty

- *14 Cows for America*
- *Fox*
- "Battle over the Pledge" (informational article)

Literary Analysis: Define loyalty based on two of these sources. What are the key components of loyalty? How did each author develop this central idea?

Argument: Based on "Battle over the Pledge," take a stand on whether students should be required to participate in the Pledge of Allegiance in school. Write an argumentative essay using information from this article to support your claim.

Central idea: The power of images

- *My Secret Camera: Life in a Lodz Ghetto*
- *Remember: The Journey to School Integration*
- World War II Posters from the National Museum of American Art

Explanatory: Each of these sources is persuasive, but in a different way. Choose one of these sources and in an expository essay explain how it persuades. What is it attempting to show you? Does it succeed? Use several examples from your source as evidence.

Narrative: Choose an image from one of these sources and write a story that incorporates the image in some way. Develop your story using narrative elements like description and dialogue.

Central idea: Encounters with the unknown

- *Encounter*
- "The Fun They Had" (short story)
- *The Wretched Stone*

Argument: In your opinion, which "encounter" described in these sources do you consider the most harmful to the human spirit? State your claim, defend it with reasons and evidence from your selected source, and refute counterclaims suggested by the other sources.

Narrative: Using *The Wretched Stone,* write a journal entry from the point of view of one of the shipmates at a specific point during the journey of the *Rita Anne.* Elaborate on your encounter with the "wretched stone" and how it has changed your life. Be sure to use information from the story as you develop your idea. Include narrative elements like description and dialogue.

Central idea: The rights of all people

- "Japanese Internment Camps: A Personal Account" (primary source)
- "In Response to Executive Order 9066" (poem)
- *Yertle the Turtle*
- "Letter from Jackie Robinson on Civil Rights" (primary source)

Literary Analysis: Using two of these sources, how does each author develop the central idea of dignity? What destroys dignity? What restores dignity? Use examples from your sources to support your thinking.

Explanatory/Research: Using "Japanese Internment Camps: A Personal Account" and "In Response to Executive Order 9066," write an essay that identifies at least three key problems faced by Japanese Americans confined to internment camps. Support your thinking with details from both sources. Conclude your essay with thoughts about the implications of these camps.

Bottom Line for Aligning Rigor and Text Complexity for DOK 4: For this Depth of Knowledge, the challenge is not just finding the right complex texts, but choosing resources that work well together. Whenever you choose one source for students to read, make sure you select at least one more that can be linked in some way so that students will have the opportunity to make meaningful text connections.

Aligning Rigor and Close Reading for DOK 4

Choosing texts that work well together is a good place to begin for Depth of Knowledge 4. But as with everything else in education, it's what we *do* with those resources that matters most. Preparing students for the rigor of DOK 4 rests on the ultimate close reading challenge: teaching high-quality text-connection lessons. The outcome, when taught well, is that working with two or more texts will lead students to insights that wouldn't have been as apparent if they had not considered them side by side.

For example, take the text set for "Friends in a time of need." The picture book *Pink and Say* easily supports that central idea. But without the story "Spaghetti" or *Mercedes and the Chocolate Pilot*, students wouldn't be as likely to recognize the many forms that friendship can take or to broaden their definition of what makes a friend.

Hence, the close reading charge for DOK 4 is to examine the components of a strong text-to-text lesson. Most likely, a lesson comparing texts will be your *third* lesson in a lesson sequence. Lessons 1 and 2 will involve the close reading of each source individually. The third lesson will tie those texts together. This approach means that students will be knowledgeable about the content of both (or all, if there are more than two) texts and will be ready to dig deeper.

The best way to recognize what "digging deeper" for DOK 4 might look like is with a virtual peek into a few classrooms where teachers and students were engaged in small-group text-connection lessons.

Text-Connection Lesson: Scenario 1

This lesson took place in a 4th grade classroom with a group of students reading approximately on grade level. The teacher had selected two nonfiction "monster" articles, one about the Loch Ness Monster and another about the Yeti. The question she posed was this: *Which animal is the most interesting?* Students were directed to underline details in the text that made the monster interesting, and in their follow-up conversation, before writing their response, they had to explain *why* their selected details were interesting.

I liked that this teacher asked students to underline details they chose and to defend their choice. This was a helpful reminder that evidence must come from the text, not background knowledge. But a couple of features of this lesson detracted from its effectiveness. Asking students to identify the monster that is "most interesting" is very subjective. It does not require accuracy or analyzing evidence. In fact, this question doesn't really require two sources to respond.

To teach an even stronger lesson using these sources, the teacher might have asked this: *Which monster is better suited to a cold climate?* Or, *Which article provides better evidence that the monster could be real?* Both queries would need use of the two texts as well as a critical analysis of specific evidence.

Text-Connection Lesson: Scenario 2

This lesson was taught in a 5th grade classroom to a group of advanced readers. The texts were two versions of *Cinderella*, one by Charles Perrault and the other by the Brothers Grimm. The question posed was this: *What is different and what is the same in each tale?*

Fairy tales are fertile ground for text-to-text connections, and there was much potential here. The Grimm version was especially complex and worthy of close reading (and also more gruesome and violent). My concern with this lesson was that identifying events as "same" or "different" does not expect much in the way of rigor for high-ability students at the end of elementary school.

A better question might have been this: *Why are these events different? (What contributes to their differences?).* A stronger lesson might have incorporated short biographical articles about the authors so that students could have drawn conclusions about the role that each author's life story played in their writing.

A fairy tale text-connection lesson for younger readers might have compared similar tales from two different cultures, such as *Korean Cinderella* by Shirley Climo and an African Cinderella story, *Mufaro's Beautiful Daughters* by John Steptoe. The lesson could focus on how setting affected other elements of the story. Students could also compare the traditional (Perrault) *Cinderella* to a modern adaptation like *The Paper Bag Princess* by Robert Munsch: *How were the main characters different? What was different about each story's message?*

Text-Connection Lesson: Scenario 3

This 6th grade lesson with a small group of students who were mostly English learners used two texts: Ruby Bridge's picture book autobiography, *Through My Eyes,* and the fairy tale "Rumpelstiltskin" by the Brothers Grimm. The question posed was this: *What are the similarities and differences between the problem in these two stories?*

I love questions like this that forge connections between two seemingly unrelated people or topics. What could a fairy tale character possibly have in common with an important figure from American history? This question was a challenge for these students, but for all the right reasons. It encouraged their creative thinking, and although everyone seemed to be talking at once, they were at least *talking*—something we don't always see with students new to English.

The reason these students had so much to talk about was because the teacher helped them understand that they needed to focus their thinking. If they stayed at the surface, trying to compare spinning straw into gold to desegregating a school in New Orleans, there wouldn't be much to say. But if they viewed the question as a series of points to consider, they would have lots to discuss.

In this case, the points the teacher provided were these: *What was the problem each girl faced? How was the problem in "Rumpelstiltskin" similar to the problem in the story about Ruby Bridges? What were the character traits (personal characteristics) of Ruby and Rumpelstiltskin, and how did these traits make a difference? What motivated the parents of each girl (what did they care about)? What were the pros and cons of solving the problem the way these parents chose to solve it?* The teacher had even provided a graphic organizer that included these focus points so students could prepare for their discussion.

The teacher began by asking students to identify the problem in each story and how the problems were similar. In both stories, the parents sent their daughter to someplace new and scary, students concluded, though the reasons were different. This point, the overall focus, didn't produce much conversation, but the next question really got the ball rolling.

Teacher:	What motivated each girl's parents?
Student 1:	In both stories, the parents wanted what was best for their child.
Student 2:	I don't think so. Rumpelstiltskin's father wanted what was best for himself. He wanted the king to pay attention to him. It says so right on the first page. (Student flips back to page 1 and reads evidence aloud.)
Student 1:	So, Rumpelstiltskin's father was motivated by greed or power. But not Ruby's.

Student 3:   I think Ruby's parents wanted their daughter to be famous.

Student 2:   But they couldn't have known this situation would, like, "go viral."

Student 4:   I think they were sick of segregation and wanted Ruby to go to a better school. See, it says right here… (evidence cited).

Student 3:   Maybe they wanted to stop segregated schools for everyone.

Student 4:   You could be right. Segregation was a huge problem in the South. Remember the book we read about Martin Luther King?

Teacher: What were the pros and cons of sending Rumpelstiltskin off to spin gold and Ruby off to that new school?

Student 1:   Rumpelstiltskin could have been killed. If this wasn't a fantasy, that girl would have been dead after the first night.

Student 3:   But remember the marshals protecting Ruby? They thought she might get hurt. That would have been a bad outcome for her, too.

Student 4:   But in the end, both girls survived and accomplished their goal.

This conversation was just getting started, punctuated with pauses after each student weighed in to cite evidence. With few prompts from their teacher, there was much dialogue, and although there may not have been a lot of consensus, that was OK. By the end of the session, all students had shared their thinking, had listened to their peers, and were ready to write a literary analysis essay responding to this same question.

Here's a short list of take-aways to enhance text-to-text close reading lessons:

- Text-connection lessons should be preceded by the close reading and discussion of each text alone to construct meaning.

- Text connections should require the active use of both (or all) sources in forming a response.

- Text connections should require evidence that is *accurate*, not just the use of details that can't really be measured (like saying something is a "favorite" or is "most interesting").

- Sometimes the *similarities* and *differences* are not enough; what is the *significance* of the similarities and differences? Why do they matter? What are the implications?

- Seemingly unrelated texts can be compared, which leads to creative, insightful thinking.

- Fairy tales offer many opportunities for comparing and contrasting, but look beyond the story elements themselves. Focus on the authors, the setting/culture, the message, the "twists"—such as setting the story in modern times, varying character traits, or changing key characters from male to female.

- A graphic organizer with focus points can be helpful to students as they prepare for a text-connection discussion and a follow-up writing task.

A powerful text-connection lesson will not only lead to deeper comprehension but will also prepare students to write—whether analytical writing (such as an argumentative essay), a literary analysis, or a story. You can lay the groundwork for this task by suggesting a few focus points. Focus will be considered more thoroughly later in this chapter, in the section on the reading-writing connections.

> **Bottom Line for Aligning Rigor and Close Reading for DOK 4:** It might appear that the work of close reading will be completed by Depth of Knowledge 4, but that would mean neglecting the greatest of all opportunities for rigor: finding similarities and differences between texts, and using those comparisons to generate critical and creative insights. This experience lays the groundwork for the biggest challenge students will face on new assessments: writing long essays or stories that draw on their comparative analysis of all sources.

Aligning Rigor and Student Interaction for DOK 4

Although it was evident from the classroom scenario about the Ruby Bridges and Rumpelstiltskin lesson that DOK 4 involves lots of kid talk, the discussion did not identify anything special about the discourse for this Depth of Knowledge. But there *are* differences to consider. At Depth of Knowledge 3, students mostly respond to specific questions posed by the teacher. Although these are open-ended and encourage divergent thinking, they are often a follow-up to a more basic question and are not intended to generate lengthy discussion. This situation changes with DOK 4.

DOK 4 typically places one question on the table, and students spend their whole-group time mulling it over—flipping between texts, tracking down the evidence they need, and sharing their thinking aloud. Let's consider what we hope to see from students as they engage in extended text talk—in addition to those criteria identified for DOK 3.

Preparation for the Discussion

Students should come to the discussion ready to talk about the identified question and the points related to the question, having read or reviewed all sources. This means we should share the discussion question and focus points with students in advance. Students' texts might be annotated or highlighted, or perhaps they've affixed sticky notes if the source is a book. They should have filled in the graphic organizer if one was provided.

Respect for Other Group Members

We can teach students the language of respect: *I agree but would like to add _____. I respectfully disagree. Did you consider _____?* These words sound good, and maybe they're sincere. But a culture of respect goes beyond scripted sentence stems. Do students willingly sit next to that boy who other students try to avoid? Do they choose him for a discussion partner? Do they offer kind or encouraging words to other group members unprompted? Students who demonstrate *real* respect toward their peers show them compassion.

Openness to New Ideas

Talking about any topic with a group of peers should accomplish one of two things: confirming our own views or modifying them. Sometimes as we discuss an issue, we solidify our original thinking because defending our point of view has led us to additional insights we overlooked initially. This is fine, and a valid outcome of a discussion. However, some students habitually refuse to acknowledge that there could possibly be another way of looking at an issue other than their own—even in the face of irrefutable evidence. This is not fine. The best minds are open minds. We want students to demonstrate a growth mindset in our DOK 4 discussions. A Rubric for Student Discourse (Figure 7.26) to measure these discussion guidelines and others identified for DOK 3 appears on page 192 in Chapter 7.

The best minds are open minds. We want students to demonstrate a growth mindset in our DOK 4 discussions.

> **Bottom Line for Aligning Rigor and Student Interaction for DOK 4:** It is at this Depth of Knowledge that the most complex conversation will take place, not just because it involves talking about multiple texts, but because the questions are broader and invite more contemplation. Build a culture of conversation in your classroom by helping students understand what it means to be a great group member.

Aligning Rigor and the Reading-Writing Connection for DOK 4

Back when I taught 5th grade, I was a whiz at teaching the five-paragraph essay. I don't mean to brag, but I'm pretty sure I could have taught Lassie to write an essay. This wasn't for sport but for survival. It was nearly a decade before the arrival of the Common Core, and at that time, the writing assessment in my state was very clear-cut. In 3rd and 4th grades, students were tested on narrative writing. In 5th and 6th grades, it was expository, and in 7th and 8th grades, persuasive. As you can imagine, teachers were hyperfocused on the one type of writing tested at their grade level. "How can we teach *all* kinds of writing in a single year?" they wanted to know when they saw the Common Core Writing standards.

By then, I had moved on to university teaching, tasked with helping candidates in our Master of Reading Program—all certified teachers—resolve this dilemma. How could teaching multiple types of writing in the same year be less overwhelming? We began by creating a chart that showed the similarities and differences between types of writing and the components of each one (see Figure 4.2).

Comparing Types of Writing

The chart in Figure 4.2 is an adaptation of information from SBAC and PARCC, with a few tweaks from me (see Performance Task Writing Rubrics: http://www.smarterbalanced.org/assessments/practice-and-training-tests/resources-and-documentation/; PARCC Scoring Rubric for Prose Constructed Response Items: https://parcc.pearson.com/resources/Practice-Tests/ELA_GR/ELA_L_Grade_4-5_July_2015_Updated_Rubric_v3.pdf. (Note that PARCC rubrics can be accessed for grade 3 and grades 6–8, too.) Several things should stand out. First, the critical components of assessed writing are the statement of purpose or focus, organization, elaboration of evidence, language and vocabulary, and conventions. You might also notice that except for conventions, narrative writing has entirely different expectations from other writing modes. We'll come back to this point later.

For all other writing, the years I spent honing students' five-paragraph essay skills paid high dividends. We're no longer looking for *five* paragraphs, but many other structural components prevail. Truth to tell, the organization, elaboration of evidence, and language components are the same across all types of analytical writing.

Similarities Among Types of Writing

When we say that organization, elaboration, and language are the same, this means that students need their informative or research writing, opinion/argument pieces, or literary analysis to begin with an introduction, include several body paragraphs, and end with a conclusion. We want central ideas to be elaborated with suitable evidence, explained with appropriate vocabulary, and organized cohesively with paragraphs that connect logically to one another.

FIGURE 4.2 | **Comparing Types of Writing**

	Narrative	**Informative/ Research**	**Opinion/ Argument**	**Literary Analysis**
Statement of purpose/focus (coherence, clarity, and cohesion)	Setting, narrator, and characters	State thesis; maintain controlling/ main idea, or compare/contrast	State claim; defend claim with reasons; address alternate claims	State thesis; maintain controlling/ main idea, or compare/contrast
Organization (coherence, clarity, and cohesion)	Logical flow	Logical flow; stay on topic; introduction, body, conclusion	⟶	
Elaboration of evidence (development of the topic)	Elaborate with details, dialogue, and description	Provide evidence from sources, specific elaboration	⟶	
Language and vocabulary (effective use of language)	Sensory, concrete, and figurative language	Precise language, right for audience and purpose	⟶	
Conventions	Follow rules of grammar, usage, mechanics, and punctuation	⟶		

No matter how you slice and dice it, a strong body paragraph is the same in all analytic writing. There's an opening sentence with an organizing idea, several follow-up sentences with details that defend that idea, and a final sentence providing a smooth transition to the next paragraph. The kinds of details might vary: facts, statistics, quotes from a character or author, text-based inferences, anecdotes, and other references. But the point is, you don't have to teach students how to write three or four different kinds of body paragraphs for three or four different kinds of writing. And because body paragraphs make up the lion's share of all analytical essays, this should be an immediate stress-reducer.

But we're not home free yet; and in fact, the beginnings of different kinds of analytical pieces deserve more attention than we may afford them. The purpose of any introduction is to clarify the thesis or main idea of the piece and to establish the focus—the points that will be addressed. The root of the problem for most students is the focus. Exactly what will they focus on in their writing? What will they choose for their key points?

Every writing task will be slightly different, but we can establish some general focus points for each type of writing. Think back to the text-connection lessons described earlier in this chapter. What made the Rumpelstiltskin/Ruby Bridges lesson so successful? It was the focus points the teacher provided to guide students' thinking. The writing task that followed was a literary analysis. The students were prepared for it because they understood the focus points to include.

These same basic focus points will apply to all text-connection lessons where the expected outcome is literary analysis. And there are some focus points for text-connection lessons that culminate in other types of writing as well, both analytical and narrative, as listed in the next sections.

Focus Points for Text-Connection Lessons That Culminate in Analytical Writing

Focus points for analyzing literature to write a literary analysis

- What is the issue? What problem are you solving?
- How did character traits matter?
- How did character motivations matter?
- How did the time and place make a difference to the situation?
- Why is this an important problem to solve? (What are the pros and cons of different solutions?)

Focus points for analyzing informational sources to write an opinion/argument essay

- What is the issue?
- Why is this issue important?
- What does each point of view claim?
- What reasons are given to support one side of the argument?
- What reasons are given to support the other side of the argument?
- Which side of the argument do you support, and what are your top [three] reasons?
- Why do you think the other point of view is wrong? Be specific.

Focus points for reading informational sources to write an explanatory/informative essay or research paper

- What is the topic?
- Why is this topic important?

- What are the most important points in Source 1?
- What are the most important points in Source 2?
- How is Source 2 different from Source 1? (Does it agree or disagree with Source 1? What new points does it make?)
- Do you trust these sources based on who wrote them and when they were written?
- What might happen in [five] years because of understanding or *not* understanding this topic?

In the past, we supported students' analytical writing by telling them to compare their sources. But compare *what*? By focusing their thinking on specific points, students now know what to compare and can move forward with their analysis. Narrative writing will benefit from focus points as well.

Focus Points for Text-Connection Lessons That Culminate in Narrative Writing

Teaching a lesson that culminates in narrative writing can be based on a literary source, an informational source, or both. The difference between this lesson and most reading lessons we teach is that this one will emphasize *how* the author writes rather than just the meaning of *what* the author writes. There are lots of points for students to consider. But look back at Figure 4.2, the chart for comparing types of writing. Narrative points affect more than the focus. These points will be important to every component of a story.

Focus points for studying informational or literary sources to write a narrative

If it's an informational source

- What details did the author provide that you might want to use in a story on this topic?

If it's a literary source

- What is the genre, and what characteristics of this genre did you find in this source?
- Who are the characters? What are their traits and what is important to them?
- What is the problem in the story? Did it get solved yet, or does it still need to be solved?
- What crafts did the author use to develop ideas?
- How do parts of the story fit together?
- What words or phrases can you picture in your mind?
- How does the author make the story sound real?
- Is there anything else about the story that stands out? Explain.

Graphic organizers to focus students' thinking for each type of writing are provided on pages 171–174 in Chapter 7 (Figures 7.10, 7.11, 7.12, and 7.13). Be sure to use these in your text-connection lessons.

> **Bottom Line for Aligning Rigor and Reading-Writing Connections for DOK 4:** There are many types of writing that can evolve as students write to sources. Teaching these writing types will be overwhelming unless we can show students that all analytical writing is more similar than different. However, we also need to help students understand the ways each kind of writing is unique, especially in its focus. Providing a focus point to students for each type of writing will get their writing off to a solid start.

Aligning Rigor and Formative Assessment for DOK 4

To align rigor with the assessment of Depth of Knowledge 4, the questions we most need to ask ourselves are these: *What kind of reader will make us proud to send on to the next grade, the next school, or eventually, the college or university? What is it that the best thinkers do with their knowledge of a text?* All states prescribe rubrics so that students' DOK 4 performance is evaluated by uniform criteria. For possible additional considerations, I suggest eight criteria, defined here, and placed into the Rubric for Extended Thinking (Figure 7.27) on page 193 in Chapter 7.

Problem/question/issue. The best thinkers clearly articulate the essential problem, question, or issue at hand, based on their reading. They probe beneath the surface to understand why a problem is significant, how it developed, and why it needs to be solved.

Openness. The best thinkers willingly examine multiple points of view from various resources with fair-mindedness and empathy. They are willing to reconsider their past thinking based on new evidence and are not afraid to recognize pros and cons, even when an alternate point of view is unpopular.

Key points. The best thinkers identify key points and big ideas and distinguish them from less significant concepts and small details. They address key points in a logical sequence.

Elaboration. The best thinkers provide full elaboration of key points with the most useful details. They sift through multiple sources efficiently, noting which facts or details will be the most powerful in supporting their main points. They also know when enough is enough, when they've made their point and can move on.

Inferences. The best thinkers make insightful, relevant inferences. They are astute observers of text and notice the small details an author provides that are clues to meaning—implied but not stated. They distinguish between clues that are essential and those that are not, and often recognize nuances that other readers miss.

Synthesis. The best thinkers integrate information logically and meaningfully. They put ideas together in ways you may not anticipate. But their reasoning shows a strong knowledge of the content. There's a "wow" factor derived from both the uniqueness and quality of the thinking.

Implications. The best thinkers recognize probable from improbable implications and predict consequences based on solid inferential thinking. What may be the outcome of a situation if it is not resolved? What next steps could a researcher advocate? The problem itself is often less significant than what will happen next.

Communication. The best thinkers write about their learning or present it in another manner appropriate to the task. Their work is carefully prepared, and it shows the individuality of the student who designed it. There is no question that it reflects all the rigor we desire from a student's literacy learning.

It's a Wrap

At the beginning of this book, I shared this definition of rigor:

> Rigor is the result of work that challenges students' thinking in new and interesting ways. It occurs when they are encouraged toward a sophisticated understanding of fundamental ideas and are driven by curiosity to discover what they don't know. (Sztabnik, 2015)

We focused then on two important words in this definition: *result* and *toward*. Throughout this book we have identified the *result* of rigor at each Depth of Knowledge:

- For DOK 1: Precision in identifying the best textual evidence
- For DOK 2: Independence in applying literacy skills and concepts accurately
- For DOK 3: Insight into content and craft based on depth of reasoning
- For DOK 4: Creativity in synthesizing information, often from multiple sources or points of view

What about that other word, *toward*? By Depth of Knowledge 4, students are no longer heading *toward* a sophisticated understanding of fundamental ideas; they have nearly *arrived*. Nearly!

Now that we've reached DOK 4, the end of the line, we recognize that there is never really a final threshold when it comes to thinking. There's always the next step, and the one after that—not to achieve tougher literacy standards, but

There is never really a final threshold when it comes to thinking. There's always the next step, and the one after that—not to achieve tougher literacy standards, but to engage the mind and the spirit in the joy of reading.

to engage the mind and the spirit in the joy of reading. What else could students explore related to the content of a text, its craft, or its emotional impact? This question applies to educators too. What else could *you* discuss related to *this* book? Wouldn't it be fun to discuss questions such as these:

- Who would benefit from reading this book?
- Is there any information here that you question or think might not be correct?
- If you were to make this book into a presentation for your colleagues, what would you be sure to include?
- How did the author make you think?
- How do you feel about this book now compared to when you first started reading it?

These questions are for you, but many like them for students are listed on pages 185–186 in Chapter 7, in Figures 7.21 and 7.22. Although the questions are all text-dependent and each could be aligned with a standard, they would be unlikely to appear on a test because they are too subjective and difficult to measure. Although test questions are *important*, all *important* questions will not necessarily appear on a test. Tuck that thought away for safe keeping.

Here's one last nugget. Now that you've poured your heart (and many hours) into reading this book and turning it into action in your classroom, check out the end of Chapter 7, Figure 7.30: The Book at a Glance. The whole book. Summarized. Your one-page cheat sheet.

Bottom Line for Aligning Rigor and Formative Assessment for DOK 4: Just as DOK 4 represents the most challenging thinking, it also exemplifies the most rigorous assessment. Students are expected to produce different types of analytical and narrative writing pieces that are the equivalent of several pages, often synthesizing information from two or more sources. Your state prescribes a rubric to evaluate students' DOK 4 performance. Additionally, the criteria defined here and in Chapter 7 in the Rubric for Extended Thinking (Figure 7.27) will guide a more comprehensive analysis of students' most profound thinking.

PART 2

Materials to Support DOK in Literacy Instruction

5

Sample Lessons and Planning Templates

All the lessons described in this chapter are close reading lessons, and they all relate to the same text, a chapter from *Black Beauty* by Anna Sewell. They are designed to show how different ways of focusing comprehension instruction can support different Depths of Knowledge. You might or might not want to teach four lessons for a short passage like this, but the same principles could be applied whether it's this chapter from *Black Beauty* or any other source.

In general, lessons for each Depth of Knowledge will emphasize a different aspect of comprehension:

- A DOK 1 lesson will address basic construction of meaning.
- A DOK 2 lesson will build or reinforce a skill.
- A DOK 3 lesson will focus on deeper insights demonstrated through oral and written response.
- A DOK 4 lesson will connect texts, first through conversation, and then through a longer writing task.

In this chapter, I share sample lessons using selections from *Black Beauty*, available from http://www.gutenberg.org/files/271/271.txt. We will draw upon the underlined passages in the excerpt later in this chapter in the section Lesson for DOK 2.

Excerpt from *Black Beauty*, Chapter 7: Ginger

> **Introduction:** *Black Beauty*, narrated in the first person, is a memoir of a handsome black horse from its early days as a colt on an English farm with his mother, to his hard life pulling horse-drawn taxi cabs in London, and finally to his retirement in the English countryside. Each short chapter tells of an experience in Beauty's life and contains a lesson. In this excerpt from the chapter about Ginger, Beauty's companion, there is certainly a lesson—or two—to be learned.

One day when Ginger and I were standing alone in the shade, we had a great deal of talk; she wanted to know all about my bringing up and breaking in, and I told her.

"Well," said she, "if I had had your bringing up I might have had as good a temper as you, but now I don't believe I ever shall."

"Why not?" I said.

"Because it has been all so different with me," she replied. "I never had any one, horse or man, that was kind to me, or that I cared to please, for in the first place I was taken from my mother as soon as I was weaned, and put with a lot of other young colts; none of them cared for me, and I cared for none of them. There was no kind master like yours to look after me, and talk to me, and bring me nice things to eat. The man that had the care of us never gave me a kind word in my life. I do not mean that he ill-used me, but he did not care for us one bit further than to see that we had plenty to eat, and shelter in the winter.

1. STOP AND REFLECT
What is the author explaining here?
What words are confusing?

"A footpath ran through our field, and very often the great boys passing through would fling stones to make us gallop. I was never hit, but one fine young colt was badly cut in the face, and I should think it would be a scar for life. We did not care for them, but of course it made us more wild, and we settled it in our minds that boys were our enemies. We had very good fun in the free meadows, galloping up and down and chasing each other round and round the field; then standing still under the shade of the trees.

2. STOP AND REFLECT

What is the author explaining here?
What words are confusing?

"But when it came to breaking in, that was a bad time for me; <u>several men came to catch me, and when at last they closed me in at one corner of the field, one caught me by the forelock, another caught me by the nose and held it so tight I could hardly draw my breath</u>; then another took my under jaw in his hard hand and wrenched my mouth open, and so by force they got on the halter and the bar into my mouth; then one dragged me along by the halter, another flogging behind, and this was the first experience I had of men's kindness; it was all force. They did not give me a chance to know what they wanted. I was high bred and had a great deal of spirit, and was very wild, no doubt, and gave them, <u>I dare say, plenty of trouble, but then it was dreadful to be shut up in a stall day after day instead of having my liberty, and I fretted and pined and wanted to get loose</u>. You know yourself it's bad enough when you have a kind master and plenty of coaxing, but there was nothing of that sort for me.

3. STOP AND REFLECT

What is the author explaining here?
What words are confusing?

"There was one—the old master, Mr. Ryder—who, I think, could soon have brought me round, and could have done anything with me; but he had given up all the hard part of the trade to his son and to another experienced man, and he only came at times to oversee. His son was a strong, tall, bold man; they called him Samson, and he used to boast that he had never found a horse that could throw him. <u>There was no gentleness in him, as there was in his father, but only hardness, a hard voice, a hard eye, a hard hand; and I felt from the first that what he wanted was to wear all the spirit out of me, and just make me into a quiet, humble, obedient piece of horseflesh.</u> 'Horseflesh'! Yes, that is all that he thought about," and Ginger stamped her foot as if the very thought of him made her angry.

4. STOP AND REFLECT

What is the author explaining here?
What words are confusing?

Why I Chose This Text

As indicated, I retrieved this passage online from Project Gutenberg (http://www.gutenberg.org/), a huge archive of e-books for texts that are out of copyright and therefore in the public domain, available at no cost to anyone. It's a wonderful collection of great stuff, particularly classic poetry, folklore, and classic children's literature. (This isn't a great site for informational texts because those sources usually need to be current and are not yet in the public domain.) The entire text of *Black Beauty* is available on this site. But for a single lesson, we want short passages for in-depth exploration. For these lessons, I chose this excerpt of about 700 words. The same passage can be used as a mentor text for lessons at various depths of knowledge.

The Lexile (see p. 8) for this passage is 1010L, perfect for 6th grade but also a good fit for grades 4 and 5 with teacher guidance. It could be used for 7th and 8th grades with students reading at or below grade level.

I picked this text for close reading because it is an example of high-quality children's literature that meets the criteria for reinforcing different Depths of Knowledge. It offers plenty of evidence, in support of DOK 1. It provides opportunities to build concepts and skills, the challenge for DOK 2. This particular passage is provocative in its focus on a controversial subject, a main consideration for DOK 3, with plenty of opportunities for written response. And there are options for pairing this text with another book or article that explores a similar theme for conversation and extended writing, the essence of DOK 4.

This text also represents numerous complexities based on Common Core criteria:

- **Knowledge demands**—*Black Beauty* is set in England in the late 19th century, a place and a time unfamiliar to most young readers. It focuses on the abuse of animals, a subject that may be familiar to students generally, though they will probably not have much background knowledge about the mistreatment of horses; they will need to get their information from the text.

- **Language**—This passage includes numerous words related to horses: *gallop, breaking in, forelock, halter,* and more. Students without knowledge of this vocabulary will need to read extra closely to infer these word meanings. Other words may be unknown as well, such as *fretted, pined,* and *coaxed.*

- **Structure**—The most obvious structural complexity of this passage—in fact, of this entire book—is its anthropomorphism; animals talk and act like people. Two horses are having a conversation. However, an added complexity is that almost the entire passage is a soliloquy, Ginger's musings about her own youth. There is no response from Beauty to gauge the significance of Ginger's words.

- **Meaning**—Much of the story addresses the mistreatment of horses in this time and place, a problem that readers will discern through their close reading. Will students recognize from this passage that Ginger's explanation of the way her upbringing has affected her present state of mind also applies to children and the way they are raised?

Lesson for DOK 1: Finding Evidence in the Text

Purpose

Students will construct meaning by finding as much evidence as possible in the passage. Remember that the goal of DOK 1 is to retrieve evidence directly from the text. Hence, this lesson will not delve into deeper meaning achieved through inferences.

Process

As a whole class or in a small group, students will read the passage independently, chunk by chunk, to find as much evidence as possible on their own. This reading will be followed by teacher-led, text-dependent questions aimed at additional evidence that students overlooked in their independent reading. Lesson length should be approximately 20 minutes.

Steps

1. Begin the lesson by reading and discussing the introduction in the text box. This can be read aloud by the teacher if desired. Try to avoid other prereading practices such as predictions, personal connections, and vocabulary frontloading that reduce students' need to read closely themselves.

2. Optional: Ask students to read the whole passage one time, just for the gist. Then ask for a general impression or for a detail that stood out. Skip reading for the gist if you prefer.

3. Ask students to read silently the first chunk of text (to the first "Stop and Reflect" box), reminding them to take note of information the author is explaining in that chunk and words they find confusing.

4. At the end of each chunk, discuss the details students found and any confusing words.

5. Ask follow-up text-dependent questions after students have shared their evidence for each chunk. Remember that questions aimed at DOK 1 should only ask for evidence stated directly in the text. (There will be plenty of inferential thinking within DOK 3 and DOK 4 lessons.)

Questions to follow Chunk 1

- How does Ginger explain her bad temper?
- In what ways was Ginger's early life a sad one? Give examples.
- Possible words to clarify: *temper, weaned, ill-used, shelter*

Questions to follow Chunk 2

- What caused Ginger to conclude that boys were enemies?
- How did Ginger's life in the free meadow compare to other parts of her life?
- Possible word to clarify: *gallop*

Questions to follow Chunk 3

- What words does the author use to show you that Ginger was in pain?
- Why does Ginger say she was treated so harshly?
- Possible words to clarify: *forelock, halter, bar, flogging, high bred*

Questions to follow Chunk 4

- How did Samson treat Ginger? Explain, using details from the text.
- What words does the author use to show Samson's treatment of Ginger?
- Possible words to clarify: *horseflesh, trade*

To use the *Planning Template for DOK 1 Lesson* (Figure 5.1) most effectively, first ask students to respond to the two prompts following each chunk of text. When students can tell you in their own words *What is the author explaining here? What words are confusing?*, they're already on the road to constructing meaning. Next, to solidify meaning, ask the suggested text-dependent questions, (or when you're designing your own lesson, questions that you've devised). Of course, you can always add other literal meaning questions for *Black Beauty*, too, if you'd like.

Tools and Resources

- I Spy Cards (Figure 7.1, page 159): Use with primary-grade students during reading.
- Finding Evidence as I Read Literature (Figure 7.5, page 166): Use with intermediate-grade and middle school students during reading.
- Finding Evidence as I Read Information (Figure 7.6, page 167): Use with intermediate-grade and middle school students during reading.
- Identifying Important Words and Details in a Text After Reading (Figure 7.7, page 168): Use with intermediate-grade and middle school students after reading or as formative assessment task. (Use with primary students if appropriate.)

FIGURE 5.1 | Planning Template for DOK 1 Lesson: Identifying Evidence

Text: _____

Text Chunk	Independent Close Reading and Evidence Questions
Chunk 1	**Independent Close Reading** What is the author explaining here? What words are confusing?
	Evidence Questions
Chunk 2	**Independent Close Reading** What is the author explaining here? What words are confusing?
	Evidence Questions
Chunk 3	**Independent Close Reading** What is the author explaining here? What words are confusing?
	Evidence Questions
Chunk 4	**Independent Close Reading** What is the author explaining here? What words are confusing?
	Evidence Questions

Lesson for DOK 2: Applying Skills and Concepts

Purpose

Students will apply the concept of paraphrasing to short segments of text to demonstrate comprehension. This passage could be used to build other concepts and skills as well. But paraphrasing is a good example of a skill lesson that could work for any text. Follow a sequence of steps like the one described below.

Process

In a small group (preferable) or with the whole class, begin the lesson by linking today's objective to the initial reading of this text. Then explain and model the skill of paraphrasing, gradually releasing responsibility to students by pausing and prompting, and providing guided practice. The lesson will conclude with a brief reflection and the opportunity to apply the skill of paraphrasing independently *after* the lesson. Lesson length should be approximately 20 minutes.

Steps

1. *Link.* Remind students that when they read this excerpt from *Black Beauty* initially, they got as much meaning as possible through independent close reading by noticing the important details and talking about words that needed clarification. Today's lesson builds on that understanding.

2. *Explain* that paraphrasing is saying something in your own words. You can keep some of the key words, especially terms that go with the topic (in this case, words related to horses), but otherwise, try to restate the idea so it sounds like *you* talking, not the author. Paraphrasing is different from summarizing. You are not trying to make the information shorter. The goal is to keep the same meaning as the author had in mind, but in your own words.

3. *Model* paraphrasing with the underlined sentences in the first chunk of text:

   Sentences from the text:

   There was no kind master like yours to look after me, and talk to me, and bring me nice things to eat. The man that had the care of us never gave me a kind word in my life.

   Paraphrased sentences:

   My master was never nice like yours. He never gave me good things to eat or even said anything kind to me.

Point out the features of your paraphrased sentences: *Notice that I kept the author's meaning—that Ginger's master was not kind to her. But my sentences sound like I'm talking, not the author. There were no words about horses I needed to keep, but I did keep the word "kind" because I thought it was a key word in the passage.*

4. *Pause and prompt.* Reread the underlined sentences in the second chunk of text. (The teacher can read this orally, or students can read it themselves, silently.)

Sentences from the text:

<u>A footpath ran through our field, and very often the great boys passing through would fling stones to make us gallop. I was never hit, but one fine young colt was badly cut in the face, and I should think it would be a scar for life.</u>

Teacher prompts: What is the author trying to show in the first sentence?

Student 1: The boys threw rocks at the horses.

Teacher prompts: What else?

Student 2: So the horses would gallop.

Teacher prompts: Where were they? Don't forget that part.

Student 3: The boys were on a path in a field.

Teacher prompts: Good. Now put it all together.

Student 4: When the boys were walking down a path through the field, they threw rocks at the horses to make them gallop, go fast.

Teacher prompts: Now let's paraphrase the second sentence here, and then put the ideas together.

5. *Guided practice.* Ask students to choose one of the two sets of underlined sentences in the third text chunk and work with a partner to paraphrase it. Students could also *write* their paraphrased sentences, which would make it easier to share responses at the end of the lesson.

6. *Reflection.* Ask students to explain the goal of paraphrasing and how to paraphrase well.

7. *Independence.* Ask students to paraphrase the underlined sentences in the last text chunk, writing their restatement so it can be handed in for checking. Evaluate students' written responses using the Rubric for Proficiency in Comprehension Skills (Figure 7.24) on page 191 in Chapter 7.

To use the *Planning Template for DOK 2 Lesson* (Figure 5.2) most effectively, recognize that the sequence of steps is designed to match those of an explicit lesson, gradually leading students toward independence. Use the guiding questions within each lesson component to identify what you will say and do as you move through the lesson. The number of minutes proposed for each part of the lesson is only a rough estimate. Try not to go beyond 30 minutes for a skill lesson.

FIGURE 5.2 | Planning Template for DOK 2 Lesson: Building a Comprehension Skill

Skill: _____

Link 1–2 minutes	How will you tie today's lesson to past learning? What have students learned recently that they could build on for today's lesson?
Explain 3–5 minutes	How will you explain the skill to students so they know the steps of the process and what will count as success?
Model 2–3 minutes	Where will you model the application of the skill close to the beginning of the text? (Just one or two examples should be sufficient.)
Prompted Practice 3–5 minutes	Where will you begin to elicit students' input to see if they are catching on? (You may need to pause and ask a direct question.)
Guided Practice 5–7 minutes	What part of the text will work for student practice? (Be sure that there are enough places where the skill can be applied; students might work alone or in pairs/small groups.)
Reflection 2–3 minutes	How will you help students articulate the steps they used to apply the skill accurately? (Try to have students provide this closure, rather than providing it to them yourself.)
Independence/ Responding to the Text 5–10 minutes	How will students show you that they can work successfully with this skill without your direct supervision? (Will it be a formative task? Will it be through additional reading in the same text, or with a different text?)

Tools and Resources

- Oral Rehearsal Checklist (Figure 7.2, page 160): Use this to help students convert an oral response to a written response.
- Authors' Crafts in Literary Texts (Figure 7.8, page 169) and Text Features and Authors' Crafts in Informational Texts (Figure 7.9, page 170): Provide these to students if the skill relates to identifying author's crafts.
- Any anchor chart: Post to alert students to all the labels that might be used regarding theme, or for more precise language for other skills, such as identifying character traits or feelings.
- Data Collection Chart for Skills (Figure 7.23, page 189): Use this to record the progress of individual students on comprehension skills.
- Rubric for Proficiency in Comprehension Skills (Figure 7.24, page 190): Use this rubric to evaluate students' proficiency in applying a comprehension skill.

Lesson for DOK 3: Strategic Thinking and Reasoning

Purpose

The purpose of this lesson is to encourage thinking beyond the literal level to help students infer the deeper meaning of the text related to both content and craft. This lesson would follow an initial close read of the text focused mostly on textual evidence, Depth of Knowledge 1. The lesson for Depth of Knowledge 2 on paraphrasing (above) could precede this one if students would benefit from that skill.

Process for Oral Response

This lesson is more of a follow-up to a DOK 1 lesson, with text-dependent questions for deeper thinking and potentially a written-response task that measures inference. First, DOK 3 questions for each chunk of text could be asked immediately following the text-dependent questions for that chunk. This would require students to return to the text right then and there to dig deeper. Or these questions could be asked in a separate lesson. In either case, you would probably choose just a few of the questions to discuss. Students could be divided into cooperative groups, with each group focusing on one or more questions. Or you could be present as students discuss the questions during small-group time. It would be less effective to discuss these questions with a whole class because some students may not participate.

Questions to follow Chunk 1

- How does the author begin this chapter? How does she set up the information that will follow?
- Based on the information in this passage, how do you think the author wants you to feel about Ginger? What does the author do to make you feel this way?
- What is the author's purpose for including Beauty in this passage, since we don't learn very much about him?

Questions to follow Chunk 2

- Why do you think the author gives you so many details about the way Ginger was treated? What does she want you to understand?
- Why do you think the author includes the details about Ginger having fun in the meadow?

Questions to follow Chunk 3

- By now you should be able to see a theme emerging. What is this theme? How is the author developing it?

- Although this is a story in which animals talk, the author makes it realistic. How does she achieve this?

Questions to follow Chunk 4

- What line in this paragraph really stands out to you? Why?
- What is the tone of this paragraph? Is it the same as or different from the tone in the rest of the excerpt? Explain.
- Do you think the message in this story applies only to animals? How could it have a broader meaning?

Process for Written Response

After discussing some of these questions, give students one question to answer in writing. For students who need more support, ask them to respond to a question you already discussed. For more capable readers and writers, select a new question. To guide students in writing a well-constructed response, provide the chart Stepping Up to Success: Answering a Question to Draw a Conclusion or Make an Inference (Figure 7.4) on page 162 in Chapter 7. To evaluate students' written responses, use the Rubric for Drawing a Conclusion or Making an Inference (Figure 7.25) on page 191 in Chapter 7. Here are some good questions for written response:

- Based on the information in this passage, draw a conclusion about how you think the author wants you to feel about Ginger. What does the author do to make you feel this way?
- Make an inference about why the author gives you so many details about the way Ginger was treated. What does the author want you to understand?
- By now you should be able to see a theme emerging. Make an inference about the theme. How is the author developing it?

To use the *Planning Template for DOK 3 Lesson* (Figure 5.3) most effectively, identify a couple of deep-thinking questions for each chunk of text that will likely pique your students' interest. If one question in each part of the text gets kids talking, you may not get to all of your questions—which is just fine. Note that you will also want to determine a question for written response. It could be one of the questions you've discussed or a new one.

Tools and Resources

- Oral Rehearsal Checklist (Figure 7.2, page 160): Use as needed for students who have difficulty translating their oral response into language appropriate to writing.

FIGURE 5.3 | Planning Template for DOK 3 Lesson: Developing Deeper Understanding

Text: _____

Reading the Text	
Text Chunk	**Follow-up Questions That Lead to Insights**
Chunk 1	
Chunk 2	
Chunk 3	
Chunk 4	
Responding to the Text	
Writing Task	

- Guidelines for Explaining and Extending Your Answer (Figure 7.3, page 161): Discuss these guidelines and provide them to students to support high-quality written responses to inference questions.
- Stepping Up to Success: Answering a Question to Draw a Conclusion or Make an Inference (Figure 7.4, page 162): Discuss these steps with students, and provide them with a copy of this graphic to write a thorough response to an inference question.
- Authors' Crafts in Literary Texts (Figure 7.8, page 169) and Text Features and Authors' Crafts in Informational Texts (Figure 7.9, page 170): Provide these to students who need reminders about crafts and features to include in their informational or literary brief-writes.
- Any anchor chart: Post to support students' use of more precise language when they answer constructed-response questions.
- Rubric for Drawing a Conclusion or Making an Inference (Figure 7.25, page 191): Use this to evaluate students' constructed response to an inference question.

Lesson for DOK 4: Extended Thinking

Purpose

Teaching a text-connection lesson is a multistep process. First you need to teach Source 1: in this case, the *Black Beauty* excerpt. You would need the lesson content for Depths of Knowledge 1 and 3. The DOK 2 lesson would be important if students were challenged by the domain vocabulary. But how could you extend the message of *Black Beauty* even further? You could combine it with a second source—literary or informational—for both conversation and an extended writing task.

Many sources are available on the topic of animal rights, the humane treatment of animals, and even animal feelings. A couple of chapter books that come to mind are *Shiloh*, by Phyllis Reynolds Naylor; *Charlotte's Web*, by E. B. White; and *The One and Only Ivan*, by Katherine Applegate. For younger students, there is also a picture book about Ivan by the same author: *Ivan: The Remarkable True Story of the Shopping Mall Gorilla*.

For this connection lesson, I didn't choose a book but instead chose the ReadWorks article "Do Animals Have Feelings?" (Lexile 870 [see p. 8], appropriate for the same grade range as the *Black Beauty* passage). It may be accessed through ReadWorks at http://www.readworks.org/passages/do-animals-have-feelings. Because the excerpt from *Black Beauty* also focuses on animals' feelings, these texts work well together. Although the *Black Beauty* excerpt pulls on the reader's heartstrings and evokes empathy with Ginger, it leaves one important question unanswered: Do animals really have feelings? From a scientific point of view, possible answers arouse some controversy. The

ReadWorks article provides arguments on both sides so students can decide for themselves—keeping in mind their new friend, Ginger.

Process for Oral Response

A good extended-thinking question for students to discuss connecting these two texts would be this:

> Based on the chapter you read in *Black Beauty* and the article "Do Animals Have Feelings?" decide whether you think animals have feelings. Remember to base your thinking on information in these sources, not outside experiences with a pet or other animal.

Students could prepare for this discussion by completing the Organizer for Focusing on Opinion/Argument (Figure 7.11) on page 172 of Chapter 7. Discussing these points would help them focus their thinking for an opinion/argument essay of their own. You may also want to evaluate students' interaction in the conversation using the Rubric for Student Discourse (Figure 7.26) on page 192, also in Chapter 7.

Process for Writing Task

Pose this scenario for an extended writing task:

> Your class has been discussing whether animals have feelings, based on an excerpt you read from *Black Beauty* and an informational article about scientists' opinions on this same subject. Now you need to take a stand on this issue. Which side do *you* support: animals *have* feelings or animals do *not* have feelings?
>
> Create an argument essay that includes an introduction with your claim; several body paragraphs with at least three reasons and evidence from both sources defending your claim, and reasons and evidence why you do *not* agree with the opposing point of view; and a conclusion with thoughts about why this issue is such an important one.

This is an example of an argument task, and although including counterclaims will not be a benchmark before grade 7 on new standards-based assessments, I never object to pushing for more rigor if it seems reasonable. You can decide whether this additional component is appropriate for your class. Evaluate students' extended thinking based on your state's prescribed rubric for an opinion/argument response, or use the Rubric for Extended Thinking (Figure 7.27) on page 193 of Chapter 7.

To use the *Planning Template for DOK 4 Lesson* (Figure 5.4) most effectively, be sure to identify more than just the *extended thinking question*. Remember that the best way you can scaffold students for a text-to-text lesson is by helping them identify points to focus their thinking. It might also be useful to determine key points from each source yourself (in case they miss some especially important ones) and the insights you hope your students to uncover.

FIGURE 5.4 | Planning Template for DOK 4 Lesson: Extended Thinking

Text: _____

Extended Thinking Question
Points to Focus Students' Thinking
Key Points for Students to Identify in Source 1
Key Points for Students to Identify in Source 2*
Important Insights for Students to Recognize as They Connect the Texts
Extended Writing Task

*Add space for additional sources as needed.

Tools and Resources

- Organizers for connecting reading and writing (Figures 7.10, 7.11, 7.12, and 7.13, pages 171–174): Provide one of these organizers to students based on the kind of sources they read and the type of writing to be completed as a follow-up task.
- Theme Comparison Chart (Figure 2.3, page 43): This is a good tool for comparing texts based on theme.
- "Dig Deep" Discussion Questions for Informational Text (Figure 7.21, page 185): This is a good source of additional questions for extended thinking about informational sources.
- "Dig Deep" Discussion Questions for Literary Text (Figure 7.22, page 186): This is a good source of additional questions for extended thinking about literary sources.
- Rubric for Extended Thinking (Figure 7.27, page 193): Use this for formative assessment to determine students' DOK 4 strengths and needs.

6

Books and Other Resources That Inspire Deep Thinking

It would be hard for me to name anything I like better about the teaching of reading than the books and other resources I read to students and place into their hands for them to read themselves. I am a children's literature junkie—and proud of it. One of my favorite parts of any literacy workshop I present or time I spend consulting with teachers is sharing new titles and watching other teachers get excited about teaching with these books, too. So many books, so little time!

In this chapter, I share some of my current literary and informational favorites. They have all been lovingly selected and are currently in print or available online. Many of the online texts come from ReadWorks (http://www.readworks .org/). ReadWorks is a large, free, curated library of short fiction and nonfiction stories and articles covering all grades and Lexile levels. It's a great resource, but it's important to know that many of the comprehension questions that accompany the texts align only to Depths of Knowledge 1 and 2.

The sources I chose from ReadWorks and elsewhere represent different genres and multiple cultures. You'll find both male and female central characters, and I've tried hard to avoid gender and other stereotypes. The texts are divided into three grade ranges: K–2, 3–5, and 6–8. However, selections may be appropriate for your primary, intermediate-grade, or middle school students even if a text is suggested for a different level.

A few of these sources are featured in the respective chapters for each Depth of Knowledge, along with a brief rationale for why it is suggested—why it is a good match for the complexity important to Depth of Knowledge 1, 2, or 3. Then all the sources come together in the chapter for DOK 4, which is all about making connections between texts.

The best part: I've used these resources with students myself, and I've seen that they are worthy of our instructional time—not just because they're good stories or great sources of information, but because they inspire rigor. The books are listed in alphabetical order within each grade range.

Books and Other Resources for Grades K–2

- *Amazing Grace*, by Mary Hoffman (picture book)—Grace's class is going to put on a play of *Peter Pan*, and Grace is hoping for the leading role. With her background in dancing and acting, she's excited to audition. But her classmates have other ideas. Grace is a girl, and she's black. How could Grace play Peter Pan? But Grace is as spunky as she is talented, and after the audition her classmates easily concede that Grace will play the role of Peter perfectly.

- *Down the Road*, by Alice Schertle (picture book)—Hettie is overjoyed when her parents allow her to walk all by herself to the general store to buy eggs for her family. This is a sure sign she is "grown up." But on the return trip, Hettie forgets about grown-up responsibilities, and the result is broken eggs. Now what will she do? How will her parents react to her carelessness? These are personal challenges faced by young children as well as their parents.

- *Eggbert: The Slightly Cracked Egg*, by Tom Ross (picture book)—Eggbert resides in the refrigerator with numerous vegetable friends until they discover that the little egg is cracked. They no longer want him around and cast him out. Dejected, he attempts to hide his crack, to no avail. Sad and lonely, he at last catches a glimpse of the clouds in the sky and realizes there are beautiful cracks in the world. After visiting sights such as the Liberty Bell and Grand Canyon, he returns to the refrigerator with renewed confidence.

- "The Goose That Laid the Golden Eggs," from ReadWorks (fable)—A man had a goose that laid an egg of pure gold every day. This made him very happy. Imagining even greater happiness if he could have all the eggs at once, the man killed the goose and cut it open. Unfortunately, inside the goose there were no eggs at all. Such is the price we pay for greed.

- *Last Stop on Market Street*, by Matt de la Peña (picture book)—With help from his nana, CJ learns to think less about the things he *doesn't* have—an iPod like his friend has and a car to go places—and more about the unexpected beauty in his bustling urban world. In the end, he learns that what's most beautiful of all is giving back to people who have even less. The last stop on Market Street is a soup kitchen where what's really served up is kindness and hope.

- "Meet Rosa Parks," from ReadWorks (informational article)—This easy-to-read article explains the incident in which Rosa Parks refused to give up her seat to a white man, her subsequent arrest, and the ensuing efforts to change unfair laws. Young students will gain a better understanding of the meaning of segregation as well as the Jim Crow laws.

- *Never Smile at a Monkey*, **by Steve Jenkins (picture book)**—In this book, young readers will learn fascinating facts about lots of wild animals—with a focus on how to stay out of harm's way. For example, never pet a platypus, because you could receive a painful jab from the venomous spurs on its hind legs. Learn even more details in the back matter that explains how animal defenses protect them from their predators.

- **"The New Kid on the Block," by Jack Prelutsky (poem), in** *The New Kid on the Block*—The author describes this new kid on the block in great detail, and readers just assume the fearsome bully is a boy—until the last line: "I don't care for her at all." Once students have realized their faulty assumption, reread the poem line by line. The poet never identifies the character as a boy. Such is the power of culture-bound expectations.

- **"Should You Be Afraid of Sharks?" from ReadWorks (informational article)**—The author of this article maintains that people are more dangerous to sharks than sharks are to people. Will students be convinced based on the evidence provided?

- *Something Beautiful*, **by Sharon Dennis Wyeth (picture book)**—A little girl is challenged by her teacher to find something "beautiful" in her world. As she looks around her neighborhood, with graffiti scrawled across doors and homeless people huddled on sidewalks, this appears a daunting task. But then a cook at the local diner proclaims that her fish sandwiches are beautiful. And others in the community declare that there's beauty in a great game of double Dutch and similar everyday experiences. The girl begins to see her life differently—and feels empowered. There's definitely something beautiful about this story. Have a tissue handy for the last page.

- *Stand Tall, Molly Lou Mellon*, **by Patty Lovell (picture book)**—Molly Lou is the shortest girl in the class, has teeth that stick out like a beaver's, and sings off-key. But thanks to the loving wisdom of her grandma, Molly Lou "stands tall" and is proud of who she is. Then she moves to a new town. Grandma is no longer close by. How will Molly Lou fend off the class bully, Ronald Durkin? In the end, Ronald's mean words are no match for Molly's self-confidence. Ronald apologizes—and reforms.

- *Those Shoes*, **by Maribeth Boelts (picture book)**—Jeremy is envious of his classmates who have cool high-top sneakers, and he desperately wants a pair of his own. His grandma takes him to a second-hand store where he finds exactly what he wants—except the shoes don't exactly fit. He buys them with his own money, but it's hard to enjoy them with his too-big feet stuffed inside. When he notices a school friend with tattered shoes, he drops the sneakers on his doorstep one evening and appreciates the new boots Grandma has bought him when it snows the next day. This is a great story about want versus need, and making good choices.

- *Turtle, Turtle, Watch Out!* by April Pulley Sayre (picture book)—This nonfiction narrative traces the life of a female sea turtle from the time it hatches on a beach in Florida to later in life when she lays eggs. In between, there are many helping hands that contribute to the turtle's survival. Children love this interesting story, while also learning a lot about sea turtles and understanding how their own "helping hands" can make a difference to the future of this endangered animal.

- "The Wind," by James Reeves (poem)—In beautiful descriptive language, the author provides clues that students need to put together to infer that the answer to the riddle is the wind. Along the way, they'll encounter some lovely images within the rhythm of the words. (Available at https://learn.weatherstem.com/modules/learn/lessons/9/index.html)

- "World Wonders," from ReadWorks (informational article)—This article offers brief explanations and illustrations of six world-famous landmarks, including Mount Rushmore and the Leaning Tower of Pisa. Which one will students think is the most spectacular?

Books and Other Resources for Grades 3–5

- "Ballad of Birmingham," by Dudley Randall (poem)—This poem about the 1963 church bombing in Birmingham, Alabama, is a great way to introduce students in the intermediate grades and beyond to this horrific event in American history. Through powerful imagery, dialogue, and other crafts, the poet combines facts with fiction to imagine the events leading up to the bombing from the perspective of one of the four girls who lost their lives.

- *The Can Man*, by Laura E. Williams (picture book)—An enterprising young boy works hard to make money by collecting cans in his neighborhood but ends up undermining the efforts of a homeless man who has been collecting cans in the same area. The two strike up a friendship of sorts. What should the boy do? The ending will make you smile.

- "A Chance for Freedom," from ReadWorks (informational article)—This is the true story of two brothers who fled their home in North Korea in search of freedom and a better life in South Korea. The article describes the perils of their year-long journey, the life they wanted to leave behind, and the opportunities that await them now and in the future. This story personalizes the plight of refugees.

- "Farewell," by Lou Gehrig (speech)—Faced with a terminal illness, Lou Gehrig can no longer play baseball, and he addresses his fans about his situation. But rather than lamenting his poor health, he speaks about how lucky he has been. Students are inspired by this unlikely but admirable point of view. (Available at http://www.lougehrig.com/about/farewell.html)

- *Freedom Summer*, **by Deborah Wiles (picture book)**—It's 1964, and a law has just been passed that ends segregation in the South. This pleases friends Joe and John Henry, who are excited about being able to swim in the town pool together for the first time. But John Henry quickly learns that it takes more than a law to change people's hearts. When the boys arrive at the pool, they discover that the town fathers have taken matters into their own hands: the pool has been filled with tar so now no one can swim.

- *Martin's Big Words: The Life of Dr. Martin Luther King, Jr.*, **by Doreen Rappaport (picture book)**—There are many picture-book biographies of Martin Luther King. What's unique are the quotes of Martin's "big" words that continue to inspire us today: "Hate cannot drive out hate; only love can do that." Students will have much to discuss from these primary-source nuggets of wisdom that capture King's nonviolent philosophy about all people living together in harmony.

- *Mercedes and the Chocolate Pilot: A True Story of the Berlin Airlift and the Candy That Dropped from the Sky*, **by Margot Theis Raven (picture book)**—This book opens with a scene from burned-out Berlin, post–World War II. A true story, it features the Berlin Airlift and a pilot, Lt. Gail Halvorsen, who dropped candy to the children of Berlin in addition to groceries and other essentials. It's a touching story that features a young girl named Mercedes and her efforts to acquire some of the candy, which she calls "sweet hope." But the greatest moment of the story really occurs in the epilogue, when Mercedes and Lt. Halvorsen reconnect quite by chance. This is a lovely tribute to the difference a single person can make.

- *More Than Anything Else*, **by Marie Bradby (picture book)**—This is another book that has traveled with me to so many classrooms! Although the identity of the main character (and narrator) is not revealed to students until the last page, this book is about Booker T. Washington and his passion for learning to read. He ultimately succeeds in the face of many hardships, and the final scene is one of pure joy. Add to this the incredible illustrations of Chris K. Soentpiet, with his clever use of light.

- "Mother to Son," **by Langston Hughes (poem)**—This poem is one of the best examples of extended metaphor suitable for intermediate-grade students that you will ever find. The mother is talking to her son about persevering despite tough times, using herself as an example: "Life for me ain't been no crystal stair." With only three stanzas, this poem can be taught in a single lesson. The dialect adds to the impact.

- *Pink and Say*, **by Patricia Polacco (picture book)**—In this Civil War story, two young Union soldiers, one black and the other white, become friends when Say, who is white, is wounded in battle and Pink rescues him. The boys make their way to Pink's home in Georgia, where his mom, Moe Moe Bay, cares for them until marauders appear and kill her. Pink is then captured as well and hanged. The boys clasp hands one last time, and Say tells his friend, "This is the hand that once shook the hand of Abraham Lincoln." Like many of Polacco's stories, this is a family story passed from generation to generation.

- **"Spaghetti," by Cynthia Rylant, in *Every Living Thing* (short story)**—A little boy is all alone in a dark city neighborhood one evening, when he finds a cat who seems equally alone. Once determined to live outdoors, the boy decides to bring the cat home with him instead. Why is this boy outside by himself in the dark of night? Where are his parents? Will he be allowed to keep the cat? This short story of just two pages raises so many questions for students.

- ***The Stranger*, by Chris Van Allsburg (picture book)**—Students love this mystery about a congenial "stranger" who arrives at a farm one fall day, demonstrating decidedly odd behavior. Who is this person? As the farmer and his family get to know him, readers will get to know him as well, through a series of quirky details that can be synthesized to reveal his identity. You'll need to read this yourself to draw your own conclusion. (Initials most likely are J. F.—if you get really stuck.)

- ***The Summer My Father Was Ten*, by Pat Brisson (picture book)**—This is one of my very favorite intergenerational stories. An afternoon of fun for a 10-year-old boy and his friends gets out of hand, as they destroy their older neighbor's garden, smashing tomatoes and tearing up plants. The friends all vanish when the dejected gentleman sees what has happened. But this boy stays around to apologize and then replants what was ruined. From then on, the boy and the old man share a pot of tomato sauce each year when the tomatoes are harvested—even when the boy grows to be an adult, even when the old man is so aged that he is confined to a nursing home. This is a heartwarming story.

- **"A Tale of Segregation: Fetching Water," from ReadWorks (informational article)**—In one short paragraph, this personal memory packs a punch. A black man and his son go to "fetch water" and experience hatred and prejudice so extreme that students will find it difficult to believe an incident like this could ever have happened.

- ***Voices in the Park*, by Anthony Browne (picture book)**—Four different voices tell their own versions of the same walk in the park, all from radically different perspectives. What *really* happened?

- **"Your Name in Gold," by A. F. Bauman, in *Chicken Soup for the Kid's Soul* (short story)**—Two sisters argue at breakfast about which of them will get to send away for the personalized pin advertised on their cereal box. Older sister Mary wins, and younger sibling Anne henceforth has nothing kind to say about her sister's selfishness. But when the prize arrives in the mail, Anne is in for quite a surprise. (Available at http://www.chickensoup .com/book-story/39544/your-name-in-gold)

Books and Other Resources for Grades 6–8

- *14 Cows for America*, by Carmen Agra Deedy (picture book)—The artwork alone would make this book a standout. But the evocative story behind the pictures will sear this narrative into readers' hearts indefinitely. This is the true story of the way one small village in Kenya responded to America's September 11 tragedy—from the point of view of the Maasai who, in a grand ceremony, symbolically "gave" 14 cows to America "because there is no nation so powerful it cannot be wounded, nor a people so small they cannot offer mighty comfort."

- *Battle over the Pledge*, from ReadWorks (informational article)—Should the Pledge of Allegiance be recited in school? And more important, is it even legal to recite it? This article looks at the issue from both sides, giving students the opportunity to weigh in with their evidence-based argument.

- *Encounter*, by Jane Yolen (picture book)—This beautifully illustrated story describes the arrival of Christopher Columbus from a Taino Indian boy's point of view. Students may find it unsettling to see historical "facts" from a different perspective. Something to consider: What do we mean by *progress*?

- *Fox*, by Margaret Wild (picture book)—Who are your real friends? This story begs an answer to that question as a cunning fox befriends a one-eyed dog and a magpie with a broken wing. Bird had become Dog's missing eye, and the dog carried the bird on his back, helping her "fly." But Fox lured Magpie away with the promise of "real" flying. And fly they did—until Fox dumped the bird off his back: "Now you and Dog will know what it is like to be truly alone."

- "The Fun They Had," by Isaac Asimov (short story)—This short science-fiction story takes place in 2157 and begins as Margie and Tommy discover a book, though they're not entirely sure what a "book" is. Tommy says the book is about "school," which prompts Margie to announce that she hates school. "School" in 2157 is a robotic device that they feed homework into, and in return, they get unkind feedback from the electronic "teacher." Margie is fascinated that back in the day, children all went to a special building where they sometimes played outside and ate lunch together. Maybe these old-time schools were not so bad. (Available at http://visual -memory.co.uk/daniel/funtheyhad.html)

- "Japanese Internment Camps: A Personal Account," by Reiko Oshima Komoto (primary source); "In Response to Executive Order 9066," by

Dwight Okita (poem)—These two pieces taken together—a personal account from a woman reflecting on her years of internment, and a poem describing a young girl's response to the order of Japanese American internment—paint a grim picture of the United States' treatment of Japanese American citizens after the attack on Pearl Harbor. (The personal account is available at https://people.uwec.edu/ivogeler/w188/life.htm; the poem is available at http://adventuresinliterature.weebly.com/uploads/8/5/7/1/8571253/in_response_to_executive_order_9066.pdf)

- **"Letter from Jackie Robinson on Civil Rights," from ReadWorks (primary source)**—In this short but provocative letter from Jackie Robinson to President Dwight Eisenhower, Robinson pleads for the government to move away from its stance asking for "patience from Negroes." Instead, he implores the president to recognize the urgency of assuring "Negroes the freedoms we are entitled to under the Constitution."

- *My Secret Camera: Life in the Lodz Ghetto*, **photographs by Mendel Grossman; text by Frank Dabba Smith (primary source)**—For four years, Grossman, a photographer and Polish Jew forced into the Lodz Ghetto, covertly took thousands of pictures documenting life in the Ghetto. The result is a chilling portrayal of Holocaust horrors and the pain suffered even by those Jews who were not deported to concentration camps. Although the photographs are captioned, the pictures speak for themselves—for example, a lone child clutching a chain-link fence.

- *Oh, Rats! The Story of Rats and People*, **by Albert Marrin (picture book)**—This author weaves science, history, culture, and folklore into an account of rats that middle school readers find both fascinating and repulsive. There are more than a few surprises along the way, with facts and statistics that are as gross as they are enlightening. And then there's more: a side of the "rat story" that makes this unsavory creature appear more friend than foe.

- *Remember: The Journey to School Integration*, **by Toni Morrison (primary source)**—This collection of photographs depicts events surrounding school desegregation in the 1960s. The images—some iconic, like the photo of Ruby Bridges being escorted into the William Frantz Elementary School by U.S. marshals, and others equally poignant but less known—are captioned with fictional dialogue that captures the emotion of this moment in history. There's so much to discuss here.

- **"Still I Rise," by Maya Angelou (poem)**—Although this poem does require some maturity to be fully appreciated, it is worth the struggle, as it illuminates the African American experience and encourages all students to ask themselves "How have my experiences and the experiences of my ancestors shaped the person I am today—and the person I wish to become?"

- **"Taking Down the Green-Eyed Monster," from ReadWorks (informational article)**—This informational article tackles an age-old adolescent issue: jealousy. How do you recognize it? Why do you feel this way? What kinds of circumstances often lead to jealousy? And most important of all: How can you handle jealousy in a positive way? This article offers insight about a personal struggle that so many middle school students have faced.

- *The Three Questions: Based on a Story by Leo Tolstoy*, **by Jon J. Muth (picture book)**—What is the best time to do things? Who is the most important one? What is the right thing to do? These are the questions raised in this Tolstoy fable adapted by Jon J. Muth—with plenty for students to contemplate.

- *The Wretched Stone*, **by Chris Van Allsburg (picture book)**—What is this "wretched stone" that glows with a strange light and turns shipmates aboard the *Rita Anne* into zombies as they sit in front of it, transfixed? Many degenerate into a lower species—until a renewed interest in reading and other creative endeavors saves them from demise. Can students put the clues together to discern the identity of this "wretched stone?" This book could be used in the intermediate grades, too.

- **World War II Posters from the National Museum of American History, from ReadWorks (primary source)**—The poster images presented in this extensive collection helped to mobilize a nation, making war aims the mission of every citizen. All Americans could contribute to the war effort both at home and at work by conserving resources, producing as much as possible, making personal sacrifices, and sharing in the "ownership" of the war. Why did these images succeed?

- *Yertle the Turtle*, **by Dr. Seuss (picture book)**—Yertle attempts to build a bigger kingdom on the backs of his loyal subjects (literally). But a little turtle named Mack, stuck at the bottom, decides he's had enough, and he rebels. This story is considered a Seuss version of the rise and fall of Hitler. Never underestimate the depth of a seemingly lighthearted adventure from Dr. Seuss!

7

Teaching Tools and Resources

Many tools and resources that support teachers and students for all Depths of Knowledge were referenced in Chapters 1 through 5. They are all provided here in a classroom-ready format, organized under seven headings for easy access:

- Tools for Students' Self-Monitoring and Reflection
- Standards-Based Graphic Organizers for Students
- Anchor Charts
- Discussion Questions for Deep Thinking
- Tools for Data Collection and Evaluating Student Thinking
- Tools for Administrators and Coaches
- Sites for Accessing Sample Assessment Items and Lexile Analyzer

Within each section I describe the tool—what it is, how to use it, and the Depths of Knowledge to which it is aligned. I have also indicated a page number where the tool was introduced in an earlier chapter, in case you want to refresh your memory about the context in which a resource might be most helpful.

Tools for Students' Self-Monitoring and Reflection

All the tools are designed for students to use during or after reading to engage actively in their reading or to reflect on their thinking process as readers. Four tools are provided:

- I Spy Cards (DOK 1)
- Oral Rehearsal Checklist (DOK 2 and DOK 3)
- Guidelines for Explaining and Extending Your Answer (DOK 3)
- Stepping Up to Success: Answering a Question to Draw a Conclusion or Make an Inference (DOK 3)

I Spy Cards (DOK 1)

Page 30

These cards can be used with primary students, struggling readers, English learners, or any student for whom something tangible would support active reading. See Figure 7.1. Here are two ways to use these cards to get started:

1. Provide a card to each student. When they "spy" a key detail in a text, they hold up a card to signal they'd like to share what they found.

2. Instead of giving each student a card, hold all the cards and distribute them one at a time to students who "spy" a key detail. You may also use other criteria for distributing the cards, such as students using complete sentences or raising a hand before shouting out the answer.

Oral Rehearsal Checklist (DOK 2 and DOK 3)

Page 58

The Oral Rehearsal Checklist is designed for students to use themselves. You could convert this to a rubric for teacher use, but with students, a simple checklist is easier to manage. Consider using an audiotape that students can play back. It will be easier for them to determine whether their answer does, in fact, sound like written language or whether it rambles like oral language. See Figure 7.2.

Guidelines for Explaining and Extending Your Answer (DOK 3)

Page 95

This is a useful tool to provide to students for safe-keeping in their literacy folder. It offers some sentence starters for the third and final component of their written response to an inference question, where they need to extend their response to show the relevance of their inference beyond the text. This is a new concept to students who have been instructed for so long that *everything* they write must relate only to the text. This new challenge asks them to integrate the evidence from the text with a global life lesson or real-world application. See Figure 7.3.

Stepping Up to Success:
Answering a Question to Draw a Conclusion or Make an Inference (DOK 3)

Page 95

To succeed with a skill, students need to know not just *what* to do, but *how* to do it. This chart shows a clear sequence of steps for how to answer a question that asks for an inference or a conclusion. Note that the inference can relate to anything—a theme, a main idea, an author's point of view, or another dimension of textual analysis. Use Figure 7.4 in small groups, give copies to students for literacy folders, or enlarge for display.

FIGURE 7.1 | I Spy Cards

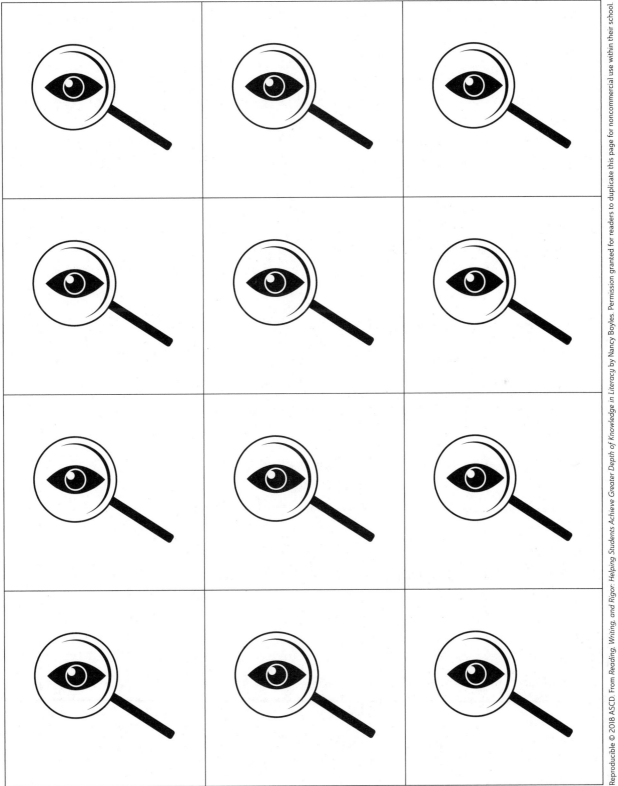

FIGURE 7.2 | Oral Rehearsal Checklist

☐ I thought about who will be reading my answer and orally explained my ideas so they make sense written down, too.

☐ I have answered the 5W/H questions (*who, what, when, where, why, how*) based on information in the text.

☐ I remembered to use connecting words like *first, next, in conclusion.*

☐ I checked to make sure I explained events in the right order.

☐ I took out confusing pronouns and replaced them with names and specific nouns.

☐ I explained words that might be confusing to someone reading my response.

☐ I thought about what else someone reading my response might want to know and tried to answer those questions in my response.

FIGURE 7.3 | Guidelines for Explaining and Extending Your Answer

Extending a Literary Text (such as a story)	Extending an Informational Text (such as an article)
· The life lesson is _____.	· [This] is important because _____.
· This teaches me _____.	· [This] is surprising because _____.
· [Being a bully] is bad because _____.	· _____ should care about this because _____.
· [Caring about other people] is good because _____.	· Something I could do to make a difference is _____.

Hints:

Using a word that ends with -ing can help you get started on the <u>extending</u> part of your answer: be<u>ing</u>, help<u>ing</u>, bully<u>ing</u>.

Try to write <u>two</u> sentences to extend your answer. Use one of the sentence starters in this chart. Then add another sentence to explain. Or you could write one long sentence that includes the word <u>because</u>.

Example: "The life lesson is don't give up until you reach your goal. If you work hard and don't quit, you can be successful. But if you're a quitter, your dreams may not come true."

Example: "Being greedy is bad. It means you get too much and other people get almost nothing, and it shows you only care about yourself."

Example: "It is important to understand that glaciers are melting because it could prove that Earth is getting warmer, and this situation could get worse if we don't take care of our planet."

FIGURE 7.4 | Stepping Up to Success: Answering a Question to Draw a Conclusion or Make an Inference

Draw a conclusion about _____. Support your answer with information from the text.*

Here is how to step up to success for this goal:

Step 1: Make sure you understand the question: What is the question asking you to do?

Step 2: Answer the question in a complete sentence. For example: My inference is _____. The main idea is _____.

Step 3: Summarize the events from the story or article in the order they happened to show how the author developed this idea.

Step 4: Extend and explain your answer by showing how the *inference* relates to a *life lesson* or how the *main* idea is *important*. The explaining/extending part of your answer should be one long sentence or two sentences.

*Examples of other questions that could be substituted include "Make an inference," "Find the main idea," "What is the lesson?"

Standards-Based Graphic Organizers for Students

These organizers are designed to be used by students during reading to support evidence of content and craft; they are useful for both literary and informational text:

- Finding Evidence as I Read Literature (DOK 1)
- Finding Evidence as I Read Information (DOK 1)
- Identifying Important Words and Details in a Text After Reading (DOK 1 and DOK 2)
- Authors' Crafts in Literary Texts (DOK 2 and DOK 3)
- Text Features and Authors' Crafts in Informational Texts (DOK 2 and DOK 3)
- Organizers for Connecting Reading and Writing (4 organizers) (DOK 4)

Finding Evidence as I Read Literature (DOK 1)

Page 26

Provide this organizer to students in the intermediate grades and above to help them monitor meaning as they read literature for evidence. This tool will work well for stories and even poetry if the poem tells a story. It will not work well for poems that do not have traditional story parts (like characters and problems). Encourage students to pause at points you have designated, or at places that they have determined themselves. It is not necessary for students to write their notes as complete sentences. A brief phrase should be sufficient—maybe a couple of bullet points. Students should use the "Words to Clarify" column to identify vocabulary that is unclear and may be interfering with meaning. It is not necessary for students to look up word meanings as they read. These notes can be used as a place to start as students discuss the evidence they have found. See Figure 7.5.

Finding Evidence as I Read Information (DOK 1)

Page 26

Provide this organizer to students in the intermediate grades and above to help them monitor meaning as they read information for evidence. This tool will work well for an informational text of any structure (main idea/detail, compare/contrast, cause/effect, etc.). It will also work for texts such as biography or literary nonfiction in which the structure is narrative but the intent is to provide information. As with the organizer for literature, encourage students to pause at points you have designated or at places that they have determined themselves. It is not necessary for students to write their notes as complete sentences. A brief phrase should be sufficient—maybe a couple of bullet points. Students should use the "Words to Clarify" column to identify vocabulary that is unclear and may be interfering with meaning. It is not necessary for students to look up word meanings as they read. These notes can be used as a place to start as students discuss the evidence they have found. See Figure 7.6.

Identifying Important Words and Details in a Text After Reading (DOK 1 and DOK 2)

Page 33

This organizer can serve as a formative task for students to complete after an initial close read. The point is to know the important words and the details in a text, because students' ability to do that shows they have constructed basic meaning. They will then probably be able to move on to deeper thinking about the text. *You* choose the number of words and details you want students to identify. You can differentiate by asking some students for *more* words and details, and other students for *fewer*. Note that a second important feature of this task is to note *why* the words and details are important. At the primary level, begin by creating this chart on a whiteboard. Provide a list of words and details that might or might not be important. Ask students to select the best words and details and to explain why each one is important. See Figure 7.7.

Authors' Crafts in Literary Texts (DOK 2 and DOK 3)

Page 60

Provide this organizer to students in the intermediate grades and beyond to help them track authors' crafts in literary texts. Is there alliteration? Hyperbole? A figure of speech? Students need to learn what authors' crafts are before they can find them. But once crafts have been explained and modeled, this organizer becomes a reminder of what to look for in a piece of literature. When students are first learning about craft, focus on just a few. I suggest the four crafts identified in the top row, as these form the essence of a well-crafted narrative: "Today when you read, see if you can find any examples of dialogue, snapshots, thought-shots, or gestures. Write the page number in the box and a couple of words from the text so you can share your craft with the class later." Add other crafts as students learn about them. See Figure 7.8.

Text Features and Authors' Crafts in Informational Texts (DOK 2 and DOK 3)

Page 60

This graphic organizer works the same way as the organizer for literature—except that informational texts typically contain fewer narrative crafts and instead use elements more central to nonfiction, some of which we call "text features." We may not think of photographs and headings as "crafts," but the author of a nonfiction article may be strategic about including them in the same way that the author of a short story may be strategic about using foreshadowing or flashback. Point out to students that nonfiction has other features they should be aware of as well, such as narrative introductions, statistics, and loaded words. See Figure 7.9.

Organizers for Connecting Reading and Writing (DOK 4)

- Organizer for Focusing on Literary Analysis (DOK 4)

Page 126

- Organizer for Focusing on Opinion/Argument (DOK 4)

Page 126

- Organizer for Focusing on Information and Research (DOK 4)

Page 126

- Organizer for Focusing on Narrative Reading and Writing (DOK 4)

Page 126

These organizers are designed to help students focus their thinking for analytical and narrative writing based on text-connection lessons. If the culminating writing task will be a literary analysis, show students how to focus their thinking as they read and compare literary sources. If the writing task will address a different type of writing, show students how to focus their thinking as they read texts that prepare them for those writing challenges. See Figures 7.10, 7.11, 7.12, and 7.13.

FIGURE 7.5 | Finding Evidence as I Read Literature

Name: _____   Date: _____

Text: _____

Chunk	Details in This Part of the Text	Words to Clarify
1	Characters, setting, problem, events or roadblocks, solution, ending	
2	Characters, setting, problem, events or roadblocks, solution, ending	
3	Characters, setting, problem, events or roadblocks, solution, ending	
4	Characters, setting, problem, events or roadblocks, solution, ending	
5	Characters, setting, problem, events or roadblocks, solution, ending	
6	Characters, setting, problem, events or roadblocks, solution, ending	

FIGURE 7.6 | Finding Evidence as I Read Information

Name: _____ **Date:** _____

Text: _____

Chunk	Details in This Part of the Text	Words to Clarify
1	Who, what, when, where, why, how	
2	Who, what, when, where, why, how	
3	Who, what, when, where, why, how	
4	Who, what, when, where, why, how	
5	Who, what, when, where, why, how	
6	Who, what, when, where, why, how	

FIGURE 7.7 | Identifying Important Words and Details in a Text After Reading

Name: _____   Date: _____

Text: _____

What words would you absolutely need in order to talk about this book?

This word in the text is important . . .	because . . .
1.	
2.	
3.	
4.	
5.	
6.	

This detail in the text is important . . .	because . . .
1.	
2.	
3.	
4.	
5.	

FIGURE 7.8 | Authors' Crafts in Literary Texts

Name: _____   Date: _____

Text: _____

Find examples of these crafts in literary text. Write the example or provide the page number in the appropriate box.

Dialogue	Snapshot (description)	Thoughtshot (internal dialogue)	Body language (small actions, gestures)
Exaggeration (hyperbole)	Figure of speech	Made-up words	Repeated words, lines, or phrases
Sentence fragments	Sentence patterns	Different font, big or bold words, italics	Words shaped in different ways or placed creatively on the page
Parentheses	Foreshadowing	Rhyming words	Flashback
Alliteration	Personification	Simile/Comparison	Metaphor

FIGURE 7.9 | Text Features and Authors' Crafts in Informational Texts

Name: _____ **Date:** _____

Text: _____

Find examples of these features or crafts in informational texts. Write the example or provide the page number in the appropriate box.

Headings	Different fonts or big or bold words	Photograph/Illustration	Text box (sidebar)
"Loaded" words	Figure of speech (idiom)	Description or descriptive words	Simile/Comparison
Narrative (story) introduction	Example that sounds like a story	Surprising or unusual detail	Statistic
Quote	Glossary	Other	Other

FIGURE 7.10 | Organizer for Focusing on Literary Analysis

Name: _____   Date: _____

Text 1: _____   Text 2: _____

What is the issue? What problem are you solving? _____

Points to Consider*	Source 1	Source 2
How did character traits matter?		
How did character motivations matter?		
How did the time and place make a difference to the situation?		
Why is this an important problem to solve? (What are the pros and cons of different solutions?)		
Other		

*Some points might not apply to some questions and texts. You may want to choose other focus points of your own.

FIGURE 7.11 | Organizer for Focusing on Opinion/Argument

Name: _____   Date: _____

Source 1: _____   Source 2: _____

Points to Consider*
What is the issue? Why is it important?
What does each source claim?
What reasons are given to support one side of the argument?
What reasons are given to support the other side of the argument?
Which side of the argument do you support, and what are your top [three] reasons?
Why do you think the other point of view is wrong? Be specific.
Other

*Some points might not apply to some questions and texts. You may want to choose other focus points of your own.

FIGURE 7.12 | Organizer for Focusing on Information and Research

Name: _____   Date: _____

Source 1: _____   Source 2: _____

Points to Consider*
What is the topic? Why is it important?
What are the most important points in Source 1?
What are the most important points in Source 2?
How is Source 2 different from Source 1? (Does it agree or disagree?) Is the focus different?
Do you trust these sources based on who wrote them and when they were written?
What might happen in [five] years because of understanding or not understanding this topic?
Other

*Some points might not apply to some questions and texts. You may want to choose other focus points of your own.

FIGURE 7.13 | Organizer for Focusing on Narrative Reading and Writing

Name: _____   Date: _____

Source: _____

Points to Consider for an Informational Source
What details did the author provide that you might want to use in a story on this topic?

Points to Consider for a Literary Source
What is the genre, and what characteristics of this genre did you find in this source?
Who are the characters? What are their traits, and what is important to them?
What is the problem in the story? Did it get solved yet, or does it still need to be solved?
What crafts did the author use to develop ideas?
How do parts of the story fit together?
What words or phrases can you picture in your mind?
How does the author make the story sound real?
Is there anything else about the story that stands out? Explain.

Anchor Charts

Anchor charts are provided here for several concepts. These charts support different standards and may be used at multiple Depths of Knowledge. Some anchor charts are useful to students because assessment items often use different words to define the same basic task. Anchor charts can help clarify this language for students. Other anchor charts are useful because they increase students' vocabulary and help them choose more precise language for ideas they are trying to express.

Display anchor charts in the classroom. Most states have regulations regarding what can be exposed on walls during an assessment, but posting these charts during instruction, before a test, is fair game. You'll find anchor charts here for the following:

- Words That Mean About the Same as *Theme* (DOK 2 and DOK 4)
- Words That Describe Character Traits and Feelings (DOK 2 and DOK 4)
- Words That Describe Tone, Attitude, and Mood (DOK 3 and DOK 4)
- Words That Describe Character Motivations (DOK 3 and DOK 4)
- Words That Describe Character Relationships (DOK 3 and DOK 4)
- Themes We Find in Books (DOK 2 and DOK 4)
- Theme Comparison Chart (DOK 2 and DOK 4)

Words That Mean About the Same as *Theme* (DOK 2 and DOK 4)

Page 20

This chart shows students the different language that may be used in a question focused on a text's central idea. Let students know that if they see any of these words in the question, the task is the same. For assessment purposes, there is no differentiation between *theme*, *central idea*, or any other term on this list. See Figure 7.14.

Words That Describe Character Traits and Feelings (DOK 2 and DOK 4)

Page 20

Students need a large repertoire of words to describe characters and people precisely. Teach the meaning behind these words, and then offer opportunities for students to use this language to describe the characters and people they meet in literature and informational sources. For example, do they know what *apprehensive* means, and whether this is more likely to be a temporary *feeling* or a more permanent *trait* of a character? See Figure 7.15.

Words That Describe Tone, Attitude, and Mood (DOK 3 and DOK 4)

Page 20

The same precision is needed for the tone, attitude, and mood demonstrated in a text. The list provided here is only a starting point. Be sure to talk about the tone and the mood of a text with your students, adding words as you need them. More important, identify characters' attitudes and how they affect other characters, the problem, or the solution to the problem. See Figure 7.16.

Words That Describe Character Motivations (DOK 3 and DOK 4)

Page 20

Although this chart says "Character Motivations," the same terms could be applied to motivations of real people in real situations. Help your students develop a deeper understanding of any text by considering how a person's or character's motivations contributed to the conflict or resolution of the conflict. See Figure 7.17.

Words That Describe Character Relationships (DOK 3 and DOK 4)

Page 20

This chart, too, can be used for both literary and informational sources. Remember that new standards focus on more than just the elements of a text. They also focus on the connection or relationship between elements. This will be especially true for the study of characters or the people central to a world event. See Figure 7.18.

Themes We Find in Books (DOK 2 and DOK 4)

Page 43

Determining the theme of a text is often difficult for students, especially young students who are not good at abstract thinking. Rather than have them invent the theme on their own, give them a few themes from which to choose. It's easier to recognize something than to produce it yourself. This chart contains too many possibilities for beginners, and some of them won't apply to texts read by younger students. Select three or four themes from which students will make their selections. Add to your list of options as you read additional sources. See Figure 7.19.

Theme Comparison Chart (DOK 2 and DOK 4)

Page 44

This chart is a nice way to continue the work with theme initiated through the chart in Figure 7.19. It not only makes theme visible to students but also sets the stage for comparing themes across texts—something essential to the rigor of DOK 4. Fill in the theme for each text as you complete it. Soon you will have two or three books or other sources with the same theme—perfect for making those text-to-text theme connections. See Figure 7.20.

FIGURE 7.14 | **Words That Mean About the Same as** *Theme*

· Lesson

· Main idea

· Central idea

· Author's message

· Claim

· Focus

· Main factor

· What is [the text] about?

FIGURE 7.15 | Words That Describe Character Traits and Feelings

· Aggravated	· Inadequate
· Agitated	· Insecure
· Anxious	· Irate
· Apprehensive	· Lazy
· Baffled	· Lethargic
· Bewildered	· Lost
· Capable	· Nervous
· Confident	· Outraged
· Contented	· Overjoyed
· Crushed	· Overwhelmed
· Dejected	· Perplexed
· Delighted	· Relieved
· Depressed	· Rundown
· Desperate	· Satisfied
· Disappointed	· Secure
· Drained	· Seething
· Ecstatic	· Shocked
· Elated	· Shy
· Embarrassed	· Sneaky
· Energetic	· Sorrowful
· Excited	· Threatened
· Exhausted	· Thrilled
· Frustrated	· Timid
· Furious	· Tired
· Heartbroken	· Trapped
· Helpless	· Uneasy
· Hopeless	· Unsure
· Hurt	· Worried

FIGURE 7.16 | Words That Describe Tone, Attitude, and Mood

- Accusing

- Awesome

- Bitter

- Callous

- Critical

- Disdainful

- Earnest

- Fanciful

- Forthright

- Gloomy

- Harsh

- Haughty

- Indifferent

- Indignant

- Jovial

- Judgmental

- Knowledgeable

- Malicious

- Mocking

- Objective

- Optimistic

- Pessimistic

- Reflective

- Sarcastic

- Sincere

- Solemn

- Thoughtful

Source: Adapted from "Words to Describe Tone, Attitude, and Mood," at https://www.vocabulary.com/lists/202236.

FIGURE 7.17 | **Words That Describe Character Motivations**

- Achievement

- Ambition

- Creativity

- Curiosity

- Desire to help community or society

- Desperation

- Fairness

- Fitting in

- Freedom

- Greed

- Guilt

- Justice

- Love of family or friends

- Loyalty

- Money

- Physical comfort

- Power

- Respect

- Revenge

- Security

- Success

- Survival/safety

FIGURE 7.18 | **Words That Describe Character Relationships**

- Antagonistic

- Best friends

- Brotherly (or sisterly)

- Close

- Dependent

- Fragile

- Friendly

- Inseparable

- Motherly (or fatherly)

- Needy

- One-sided

- Respectful

- Rivals

- Romantic

- Supportive

FIGURE 7.19 | Themes We Find in Books

· Never give up on your dreams.

· Stand up for what is important to you.

· Accept others' differences.

· Discrimination hurts!

· Honesty is the best policy.

· You can find beauty where you least expect it.

· Overcoming challenges takes perseverance.

· Building relationships takes time and effort.

· Growing up means learning to take responsibility.

· Never lose hope.

· Cultural traditions are important.

· Home is where the heart is.

· You can hold onto memories in many ways.

· There's a delicate balance between tradition and change.

· There is a circle of life.

· Words are powerful in both solving and creating problems.

· Be true to yourself.

· Honor your elders.

· Hard work pays off.

· Don't take advantage of people.

· Know when (and when not) to take a risk.

FIGURE 7.20 | Theme Comparison Chart

Theme	Book 1	Book 2	Book 3	Book 4

Note: Theme could be replaced with *character traits, motivations, problems, setting,* or other text elements.

Discussion Questions for Deep Thinking

These two lists of questions provide additional opportunities for rigor for students who thrive on a higher-level discourse. When you want to get beyond the questions asked on assessments, or if you just need a break from assessment-driven items, introduce a few of these queries. Most of them focus on a single text rather than multiple sources, but they will surely inspire some original thinking.

- "Dig Deep" Discussion Questions for Informational Text
- "Dig Deep" Discussion Questions for Literary Text

"Dig Deep" Discussion Questions for Informational Text (DOK 4)

Page 147

These questions about the content, craft, and emotional impact of an informational text are generally intended for discussion, but some could be appropriate for a written response as well. See Figure 7.21.

"Dig Deep" Discussion Questions for Literary Text (DOK 4)

Page 147

These questions about the content, craft, and emotional impact of a literary text are generally intended for discussion. However, some could be appropriate for a written response as well. See Figure 7.22.

FIGURE 7.21 | "Dig Deep" Discussion Questions for Informational Text

Content

· What do you predict will happen in five years as a result of _____?

· If you could ask only three questions about this information to test a reader's understanding, what do you think would be most important to ask?

· What words stood out to you as important to understanding this information?

· Were there any photographs, illustrations, charts, graphs, or diagrams that you thought were especially important? Select one and show what you learned from it.

· Is there any information here that you question or think might not be correct? Explain.

· Do you find the author's evidence convincing? Explain.

· Where could you look for more information on this topic?

· How did this new information add to or change your thinking about this subject?

· How can you use this information to better understand or solve an issue or problem in our community/world?

· What else would you like to learn about this topic?

Craft

· What kind of research do you think the author had to do to write this book?

· What questions would you ask the author if you had the chance to meet him or her?

· Was there anything in the way this text was written or presented that made it easy or difficult to understand? Explain.

· Does the author try to persuade you in any way? How?

Impact

· What surprised you? Why?

· What information from this text seems most important to share with someone else? Why?

· Did the reading leave you with any unanswered questions? What are they?

· Would this be a useful/interesting text for older readers? Younger readers? Explain.

· Who would benefit from reading this book/article?

· What did you agree with (or disagree with) in this text? Why?

· How did you connect to the piece? Was it personal? Was it an issue that affects your community? The world? Explain.

· What is the most interesting thing you read? Why?

· Would you like to read more books on this topic? Why or why not?

FIGURE 7.22 | "Dig Deep" Discussion Questions for Literary Text

Narrative Elements

· What if this situation or the main character existed in your life?

· What characters did you learn the most from? What did you learn?

· How did [Character's] actions affect other characters or the problem in this story?

· Which traits of the characters did you find were most like you? Least like you? Why?

· Based on what you've read so far, how do you think the story is going to end?

· Based on what you've read, what do you predict will happen next?

· What is the most interesting (or significant) part of the story?

· Did you find the story predictable? Why or why not?

· What passage really stands out? Why?

· How is the setting significant to the story?

· Compare this book or selection to another one you have read recently. What are the most important points of comparison?

· If this story were made into a movie or television show, what would need to change?

· Were the events in the selection realistic? Why or why not?

· If you could rewrite part of this story, what changes would you make? Why?

· How can you apply the theme to your own life?

Craft

· What authors' crafts most contributed to your enjoyment of this book?

· What do you think the author researched or experienced to write this story?

· What did the author do to keep you reading?

· How did the author make you think? Feel?

· How would you describe the author's style of writing?

· What did the author do to keep you reading?

· What features of this author's writing would you like to incorporate in your own writing?

· What type of person do you think the author might be? Why?

Impact

· How do you feel about the story now compared to when you first started reading it?

· Describe your overall feelings after reading this book.

· Would you encourage someone else to read this book? Why or why not?

· In what ways did your thinking change from reading this story?

· What did you learn from this book?

· Did your thinking change as you read this selection?

· On a scale of 1–10, with 10 being the highest, how would you rate this selection? Explain.

· In what ways is this selection similar to or different from what you usually read?

· If you owned a bookstore, would you stock this selection? How would you promote the sale of it to your customers?

Tools for Data Collection and Evaluating Student Thinking

Teachers collect data on their students every time they meet with them in a small group, listen to them respond in a class discussion, or interact with them in any way. Our teacher radar is always attuned to incoming nuggets of information that could provide us with clues to make our instruction a better fit for individual learners. We make those decisions on the spot and keep going amid the flurry of day-to-day classroom life. But sometimes we want to be more systematic. We want to take the time to look at our students' performance more deliberately, from different angles, to find surprises we may not have anticipated or confirmation of hunches we suspected might be true.

These are tools to make your data collection and analysis more meaningful. Note that there is no rubric for Depth of Knowledge 1. With answers that come directly from the text, there is no gray area to evaluate. Included here to measure and record students' performance at other Depths of Knowledge are a data collection chart and four rubrics. Note that the rubrics do not call for a composite score. For assessment that informs instruction, the focus should be on the individual criteria, the rubric components listed down the left-hand column—specific areas where students are strong or where they need additional support.

- Data Collection Chart for Skills (DOK 2)
- Rubric for Proficiency in Comprehension Skills (DOK 2)
- Rubric for Drawing a Conclusion or Making an Inference (DOK 3)
- Rubric for Student Discourse (DOK 3 and 4)
- Rubric for Evaluating Students' Extended Thinking (DOK 4)

Data Collection Chart for Skills (DOK 2)

Page 64

We need a way to track students' DOK 2 progress with comprehension skills, and this simple tool will get the job done. Identify the standards-based skill for each student, the difficulty of the text, and the student's level of independence in applying the skill. A quick glance will let you know whether you've exposed students to a broad enough range of standards, and if students are becoming more independent—the true indicator of a skill well learned. See Figure 7.23.

Rubric for Proficiency in Comprehension Skills (DOK 2)

Page 139

This rubric goes deeper than the Data Collection Chart in analyzing a student's skill performance. It breaks down the process of responding to a skill-related question into all of the components where a student might veer off track: Does she understand what "text structure" means, if that is the concept? Does she understand what the question is asking? Does she approach the task logically to retrieve evidence? Is her answer accurate? How much help did she need to succeed? If we don't know where the student went astray and then take steps to solve the problem, the same error may occur over and over. See Figure 7.24.

Rubric for Drawing a Conclusion or Making an Inference (DOK 3)

Page 142

For Depth of Knowledge 3, many new assessments will ask students to draw a conclusion (or make an inference). It might be about the theme or main idea of the text, but it could also relate to another standard, such as understanding character or author's purpose. This simple, three-part rubric measures what new assessments are looking for. Pay special attention to the third criterion: "Extension/Explanation." For the Common Core, we generally expect everything students write to be evidence-based; they get their information from somewhere within the text. But for this final DOK 3 criterion, the expectation is different. Students must begin with their text-based evidence but then reach beyond the page to make a meaningful connection to a life lesson or real-world application. See Figure 7.25.

Rubric for Student Discourse (DOK 3 and DOK 4)

Page 121

Engaging productively in conversation about text is more art than skill. Perhaps we cannot "teach" these principles the same way we teach students to make an inference or find a main idea. But we can make sure we talk about these points and model them when needed. How do you show that you are listening attentively? How do you build on someone's idea? Share these criteria with students, and encourage them to use this rubric to evaluate themselves at the end of a discussion. See Figure 7.26.

Rubric for Extended Thinking (DOK 4)

Page 126

There are so many possibilities for an extended thinking task that it's difficult to capture them all in a single rubric. Based on the DOK 4 product your students generate, you may want to customize the criteria you use to evaluate it, choosing some of the criteria I've identified and adding other descriptors of your own. Most extended (or performance-based) tasks begin with a problem, an issue, or a question, so a thorough understanding of this would always be important. See Figure 7.27.

FIGURE 7.23 | Data Collection Chart for Skills

Student: _____   Date: _____

Standard	Skill	Level of Independence: I = Independent, WS = With Support, R = Reteach			Difficulty of Text: H = Hard, M = Moderate, E = Easy		
		Level of Independence			**Difficulty of Text**		
		I	**WS**	**R**	**H**	**M**	**E**
1							
2							
3							
4							
5							
6							
7							
8							

FIGURE 7.24 | Rubric for Proficiency in Comprehension Skills

Name: _____   Date: _____

Skill: _____

Text: _____

Difficulty of Text: H = Hard; M = Moderate; E = Easy

Task: _____

	2 Exemplary	1 Developing	0 Not Present
Understands the concept behind the skill	Can explain the concept (such as *What is a theme?*) in a way that shows solid understanding of the term; may be able to compare this term to others that are similar, such as *lesson* or *main idea.*	Shows a general understanding of the concept, but cannot easily differentiate it from other terms that are similar.	Does not seem to grasp the concept.
Restates question in his/her own words	Can paraphrase the skill question showing suitable command of the academic language and purpose of the task.	Can articulate the question, but much of the language comes from the question itself; not much paraphrasing.	Does not seem to understand the question, mostly pulling out random words and phrases.
Uses a logical set of steps to retrieve the evidence needed for a skill	Demonstrates a logical progression of steps in reading to retrieve evidence to apply the skill; finds the *best* evidence.	Does not have a clear strategy for retrieving evidence, and some of the evidence is quite general or is not the *best* evidence.	Seems to choose random pieces of evidence, or retrieves very little evidence of any kind.
Applies the skill accurately	Uses steps for retrieving evidence to produce a *correct* response with good choice of elaborative details.	The response is generally correct but could be more elaborated, with better choice of details.	The response is incorrect or includes almost no elaborative details.
Applies the skill independently	Completes tasks related to this skill *independently* when the reading material is developmentally appropriate.	Needs occasional teacher support to complete the task.	Needs much teacher guidance to complete tasks.

Skill strengths: _____

Skill needs: _____

FIGURE 7.25 | Rubric for Drawing a Conclusion or Making an Inference

Name: _____   Date: _____

Text: _____

	2 **Exemplary**	1 **Developing**	0 **Not Present**
Inference	The inference is stated accurately.	The inference just restates the question.	No inference is stated, or the inference is incorrect.
Development of ideas	Enough details are provided and show the development of **the theme over the course of the text** (summary of text); uses one or two direct quotes in addition to paraphrased thoughts.	One or two details are mentioned, or the details are very general, or they don't support the theme.	No specific details from the text are provided.
Extension/Explanation	The extension is suitably elaborated and shows insight (an important life lesson or implication).	The extension basically restates the initial inference—no real extension or application is provided.	No extension or explanation is included.

Areas of strength: _____

Areas of need: _____

FIGURE 7.26 | Rubric for Student Discourse

Student: _____   Date: _____

	2 Exemplary	1 Developing	0 Not Present
Demonstrates preparation for the discussion	Participation in the discussion demonstrates close reading of the text, with many specific text references.	Student has clearly read the text but does not cite many specific details.	Student does not appear to have read or understood the text; does not refer to specific textual details; references do not make sense.
Listens attentively to peers to build on their ideas	Shows genuine interest in peers' responses; integrates past comments with own comments and may pose additional questions to a speaker.	Generally focused on response of speaker; sometimes appears distracted or too eager to state own point of view; may change topic back to own interest.	Does not pay attention to the speaker; off-task or too focused on sharing own ideas; follow-up comments have nothing to do with preceding conversation.
Highly interactive; volunteers ideas, but does not monopolize discussion	Consistently contributes insightful comments and ideas with good sense of how much talking is appropriate.	Sometimes contributes to discussion, but contributions do not show much critical thinking; may try to participate too much.	Seldom participates—even when called on by the teacher; very passive or even disruptive.
Respects opinions of peers; shows compassion	Waits until the previous speaker is finished; encourages and supports others, even when disagreeing.	Generally respectful, but sometimes interrupts speaker or behaves in a negative way.	Interrupts frequently; becomes argumentative when disagreeing; needs to show more compassion to peers.
Rethinks opinion based on ideas of other group members	Synthesizes information from multiple sources in order to develop more informed opinion.	Sometimes willing to change stance based on input from group members.	Emphatically defends own stance despite conflicting evidence.

Areas of strength: _____

Areas of need: _____

FIGURE 7.27 | Rubric for Extended Thinking

Name: _____   Date: _____

Task: _____

	2 Exemplary	1 Developing	0 Not Present
Articulates problem/ question/issue	Clearly articulates the essential problem, question, or issue; sees beneath the surface.	Identifies the core problem, question, or issue, but perception lacks depth.	Does not recognize the core problem, question, or issue, or only sees superficial elements.
Demonstrates openness to multiple points of view	Willingly examines multiple points of view from various resources with fair-mindedness and empathy.	Recognizes and listens to opposing points of view.	Cannot get past her/his own point of view when examining an issue.
Understands key points	Identifies all of the key points and big ideas.	Identified points are a mix of key ideas and smaller details.	Unable to identify key points, or sees no distinction between main concepts and small details.
Elaborates fully on key points	Provides full elaboration of key points with the most useful details.	Provides adequate elaboration but could be more specific in some cases.	Elaboration is inadequate, too general.
Makes inferences	Makes insightful, relevant inferences.	Inferences are relevant but lack depth of thinking/insight.	Is not able to infer, or inferences are irrelevant.
Synthesizes information	Integrates information in a logical and meaningful way.	Integrates information, but relationship between ideas is not always clear or logical.	Integration of information is weak, or there is no attempt to integrate sources.
Recognizes implications	Recognizes probable versus improbable implications; predicts consequences based on solid inferential thinking.	Sees probable implications but does not elaborate on predictions using solid inferences.	Does not recognize the likely outcome of a situation; predictions are not based on reasonable inferences.
Communicates ideas effectively in final product	Writing or other form of presentation is appropriate to the task, carefully prepared, and shows the individuality of the student who designed it.	Writing or other form of presentation is appropriate, with generally careful preparation; product is not unique.	Writing or other form of presentation is below expectation, carelessly prepared, and in need of greater personal effort.

Areas of strength: _____

Areas of need: _____

Tools for Administrators and Coaches

The tools and resources provided in this chapter to this point have supported teachers and students. But there are roles for coaches and administrators as well. At the beginning of the process, coaches and administrators can guide teachers by helping them analyze assessment items for all the information they contain and the insights they imply. At the end of the process, coaches and administrators can examine the tasks teachers provide to students to gauge the rigor they expect. Two protocols will help to achieve these goals:

- Protocol for Analyzing Assessment Items (DOK 1, 2, 3, and 4)
- Protocol for Monitoring and Supporting Instruction for Deep Thinking (DOK 1, 2, 3, and 4)

Protocol for Analyzing Assessment Items (DOK 1, 2, 3, and 4)

Page 5

This protocol is intended to be used by teachers to reflect on the kinds of questions students answer on standards-based assessments. The questions could be either selected response or constructed response, and they could be items devised by the teacher or sample items from published assessments.

For any item, first identify the standard so you know what you're measuring. This will probably be Reading, but it could also be Writing, Language, Speaking/Listening, or Research. Next, identify the Depth of Knowledge to clarify the rigor expected of students. Is there academic language that might get in the way of students' understanding? Highlight those words and phrases, and remember to discuss them with your students before they respond. Next come the most important reasons we're analyzing these items: so we can identify the skills students need to thrive on an item and the instructional strategies and resources that will build those skills. See Figure 7.28.

Protocol for Monitoring and Supporting Instruction for Deep Thinking (DOK 1, 2, 3, and 4)

Page 11

I have made the point repeatedly in this book that the rigor is in the answer, not in the question. But it is also true that teachers need to provide opportunities for students to demonstrate rigor if we hope to challenge student thinking at different Depths of Knowledge. This protocol offers coaches and administrators guidelines for what to look and listen for when observing a comprehension lesson, follow-up questions to ask about practices that may have been unclear, space for recording observations, and suggestions for supporting teachers for each DOK. Although administrators might use this protocol for evaluative purposes, coaches could use the same form for reflecting together with teachers and providing feedback in nonjudgmental ways. See Figure 7.29.

FIGURE 7.28 | **Protocol for Analyzing Assessment Items**

Standard: _____   **DOK:** _____

Text: _____

The Question and Academic Language	What are we teaching?	How are we teaching it?
The Question:	Skill or concept:	Strategy:
Academic Language:		Resource(s):

FIGURE 7.29 | Protocol for Monitoring and Supporting Instruction for Deep Thinking

Instructor: _____   Observer: _____   Date: _____

DOK and Task	Look and Listen for	Questions to Ask	Observations	Possible Supports
DOK 1 Task	· The task asks students to identify specific evidence that requires returning to the text. · The text is accessible to all students. · The teacher holds students accountable for precision and accuracy. · The teacher provides quick and honest feedback.	· What is the task and why is it appropriate for DOK 1? · Why did you select this text? · How do you think students did on this task? What is the evidence? · What did you do to support students when they had trouble identifying the right evidence?		· Help teachers select text appropriate to the task and students' reading capacity. · Show teachers how to model returning to the text for evidence. · Suggest plan for tracking data to monitor students' DOK 1 performance. · Other:
DOK 2 Task	· The task requires students to apply a skill or a concept accurately. · The text is appropriate to the skill taught. · There is evidence that skill instruction is happening in small groups. · There is evidence of gradual release toward independence.	· What is the task and why is it appropriate for DOK 2? · Why did you select this text? · How do you think students did on this task? What is the evidence? · How are you moving students toward independence? · How do you support students who are "stuck" on a skill?		· Help teachers select text that is a good match for a skill. · Help teachers implement *all* steps of the gradual-release model. · Help teachers establish small-group routines. · Help teachers know how/when to reteach a skill. · Other:
DOK 3 Task	· The task requires inference and explanation of thinking. · The text is provocative and generates discussion. · There is evidence of conversation in which students explain thinking.	· What is the task and why is it appropriate for DOK 3? · Why did you select this text? · How do you think students did on this task? What is the evidence? · How do you teach your students to explain or extend their thinking?		· Help teachers select text that generates conversation. · Give teachers strategies for helping students explain their reasoning. · Help teachers score written responses accurately.

FIGURE 7.29 | (*continued*)

Instructor: _____   Observer: _____   Date: _____

DOK and Task	Look and Listen for	Questions to Ask	Observations	Possible Supports
DOK 3 Task— (*cont.*)	· There is evidence of written response and use of a rubric for scoring criteria.	· How do you generate discourse among students? · How do you support written response for this DOK?		· Help teachers understand how to use written responses to inform next instructional steps. · Other:
DOK 4 Task	· The task requires integrating multiple sources. · The texts provide valid connection points. · There is evidence that students have been taught to compare texts. · There is evidence of longer writing pieces with a focus on different kinds of writing—scored with an appropriate rubric.	· What is the task and why is it appropriate for DOK 4? · Why did you select these texts? · How do you think students did on this task? What is the evidence? · How do you teach your students to use multiple texts effectively? · How do you support writers learning various writing modes (narrative, research, etc.)?		· Help teachers select two or more texts that work well together—including a valid connection point. · Give teachers strategies for teaching students to connect texts. · Give teachers strategies for teaching various modes of writing. · Help teachers use students' writing pieces to plan next instructional steps. · Other:

Other considerations:

_____   The teacher accurately identifies the DOK for the task.

_____   The teacher offers sufficient opportunities for DOK 3 and DOK 4 tasks.

_____   The teacher chooses text that is adequately complex, but in an appropriate range for her/his students.

_____   The teacher provides *instruction* before providing a *task*.

_____   The teacher has an accurate view of student performance.

_____   Other: _____

Key points for feedback to teacher: _____

_____

Sites for Accessing Sample Assessment Items and Lexile Analyzer

Sample Assessment Items

- Smarter Balanced Resources and Documentation
http://www.smarterbalanced.org/assessments/practice-and-training-tests/resources-and-documentation/

- STAAR Released Test Items
http://tea.texas.gov/Student_Testing_and_Accountability/Testing/State_of_Texas_Assessments_of_Academic_Readiness_(STAAR)/STAAR_Released_Test_Questions/

- PARCC Released Items
https://parcc-assessment.org/practice-tests/

- English Language Arts Practice Tests
http://mcas.pearsonsupport.com/tutorial/practice-tests-ela/

- ACT Aspire Exemplar Items
https://www.discoveractaspire.org/assessments/test-items/

- Measured Progress Item Samplers—Aligned to PARCC
http://go.measuredprogress.org/item-samplers-parcc

- Measured Progress Item Samplers—Aligned to Smarter Balanced
http://go.measuredprogress.org/item-samplers-smarter-balanced

Lexile

- Lexile Analyzer: https://lexile.com/analyzer/

This Book at a Glance

Figure 7.30 provides an at-a-glance view of this entire book. With each Depth of Knowledge specified by column, and literacy-related elements aligned to each DOK across rows, it is easy to compare one Depth of Knowledge to another. For example, how does the rigor of close reading at DOK 1 compare to the rigor of close reading at DOK 2? What should we keep in mind for the rigor of formative assessment at DOK 3, and how is that different from assessment rigor at DOK 4? Check the basics using this chart. Then return to the related chapter for each Depth of Knowledge for more review if you need it.

FIGURE 7.30 | The Book at a Glance

	DOK 1	DOK 2	DOK 3	DOK 4
Underlying Principle	Recalling and reproducing information	Applying skills or knowledge of concepts	Employing strategic thinking and reasoning	Using extended thinking
Measuring This Depth of Knowledge on Standards-Based Assessments	Focus on Reading Standard 1	Focus on Reading Standards 2–5	Focus on Reading Standards 2–8 and Writing Standards 4–5	Focus on Reading Standard 9 and Writing Standards 1–3
Aligning Rigor and Standards	Monitor basic understanding before expecting deeper thinking.	Particular challenges include Reading Standard 5 and the academic language of questions.	Remember to include follow-up questions after a more basic (DOK 2) question.	Teach the similarities and differences between components of writing: analytical and narrative.
Aligning Rigor and Text Complexity	Choose texts that intrigue students.	Choose texts that are complex in knowledge demands, meaning, language, and structure.	Choose texts that are ambiguous, provocative, or personally or emotionally challenging.	Choose texts that work well together based on a common connection point.
Aligning Rigor and Close Reading	Focus close reading lessons on finding evidence.	Focus close reading lessons on building comprehension skills using the gradual-release model.	Focus close reading lessons on inferential questions and conversation.	Focus close reading lessons on making text connections.
Aligning Rigor and Student Interaction	Keep students actively engaged during reading.	Emphasize oral rehearsal before written response.	Emphasize active participation and active listening.	Build a sense of community through extended conversation.
Aligning Rigor and the Reading-Writing Connection	Persist until a written answer is accurate.	Make sure that students can recognize crafts as they read.	Teach students to incorporate crafts into their own writing.	Teach text-connection lessons that include focus points for types of writing.
Aligning Rigor and Formative Assessment	Assess by identifying key words and details.	Assess comprehension skills.	Assess with written response that asks students to make an inference.	Assess by asking students to write full essay or story based on sources.

Appendix: Bibliography of Student Resources

American Museum of Natural History. (2015). The goose that laid the golden eggs. *ReadWorks*. Retrieved from https://www.readworks.org/article/The-Goose-That-Laid-the-Golden -Eggs/6d7bcd67-a209-45b5-88af-81040b36dbc6#!articleTab:content/

Angelou, M. (1978). Still I rise [poem]. In M. Angelou, *And still I rise*. New York: Random House.

Asimov, I. (1954, February). The fun they had. *Magazine of Fantasy and Science Fiction, 6*(2), 125.

Bartone, E. (1997). *Peppe the lamplighter*. New York: HarperCollins.

Bauman, A. F. (2012). Your name in gold. In J. Canfield, M. V. Hansen, & P. Hansen (Eds.), *Chicken soup for the kid's soul*. New York: Simon & Schuster. Retrieved from http://www.chicken soup.com/book-story/39544/your-name-in-gold

Boelts, M. (2009). *Those shoes*. Somerville, MA: Candlewick Press.

Bradby, M. (1995). *More than anything else*. New York: Orchard Books.

Bridges, R. (1999). *Through my eyes*. New York: Scholastic.

Brisson, P. (1999). *The summer my father was ten*. Honesdale, PA: Boyds Mills Press.

Browne, A. (2001). *Voices in the park*. New York: DK Publishing.

Bryner, J. (2012, September 15). What's the difference between alligators and crocodiles? *Live -Science*. Retrieved from http://www.livescience.com/32144-whats-the-difference-between -alligators-and-crocodiles.html

Buyea, R. (2011). *Because of Mr. Terupt*. New York: Random House.

Climo, S. (1996). *The Korean Cinderella*. New York: HarperCollins.

Deedy, C. A. (2009). *14 cows for America*. Atlanta: Peachtree.

De la Peña, M. (2015). *Last stop on Market Street*. New York: Putnam's.

Dr. Seuss. (1958). *Yertle the turtle and other stories*. New York: Random House.

Gehrig, L. (n.d.). Farewell [speech]. Retrieved from *LouGehrig.com* at http://www.lougehrig.com /about/farewell.html

Gilder Lehrman Institute of American History. (2016). WWII Posters from the National Museum of American History. *ReadWorks*. Retrieved from https://www.readworks.org/article/WWII -Posters-from-the-National-Museum-of-American-History/d8560d61-cce9-4f9d-98e6 -d32d7df9b5d2#!articleTab:content/

Grimm, The Brothers. (2013). *An illustrated treasury of Grimm's fairy tales: Cinderella, Sleeping Beauty, Hansel and Gretel and many more classic stories*. Edinburgh, UK: Floris Books.

Grossman, M., & Smith, F. D. (2000). *My secret camera: Life in a Lodz ghetto*. Boston: HMH Books for Young Readers.

Hoffman, M. (1991). *Amazing Grace*. New York: Dial Books.

Hughes, L. (1994). Mother to son [poem]. In A. Rampersad & D. Roessel (Eds.), *The collected poems of Langston Hughes*. New York: Vintage.

Jenkins, S. (2011). *Never smile at a monkey: And 17 other important things to remember.* Boston: HMH Books for Young Readers.

Komoto, O. (1997). Japanese internment camps: A personal account. Retrieved from the University of Wisconsin, Eau Claire at http://people.uwec.edu/ivogeler/w188/life.htm

Lovell, P. (2001). *Stand tall, Molly Lou Melon.* New York: Putnam's.

Marrin, A. (2014). *Oh, rats! The story of rats and people.* London: Puffin Books.

Morrison, T. (2004). *Remember: The journey to school integration.* Boston: HMH Books for Young Readers.

Munsch, R. (1981). *The paper bag princess.* North York, Ontario: Annick Press.

Muth, J. (1994). *The three questions: Based on a story by Leo Tolstoy.* New York: Scholastic.

Okita, D. (2015, February 28). In response to executive order 9066. *National Park Service.* Retrieved from https://www.nps.gov/manz/learn/education/dwight-okita.htm

Perrault, C., & Koopmans, L. (2002). *Cinderella.* New York: North-South Books.

Polacco, P. (1994). *Pink and Say.* New York: Philomel Books.

Prelutsky, J. (2013). The new kid on the block [poem]. In J. Prelutsky, *The new kid on the block.* New York: Greenwillow Books.

Queen Rania of Jordan Al Abdullah, with K. DiPucchio. (2010). *The sandwich swap.* New York: Disney-Hyperion Books.

Randall, D. (2009). The ballad of Birmingham [poem]. In J. E. Gardner, B. Lawn, J. Ridl, & P. Schakel (Eds.), *Literature: A portable anthology* (2nd ed.), 588–589. New York: St. Martin's.

Rappaport, D. (2007). *Martin's big words: The life of Dr. Martin Luther King, Jr.* New York: Hyperion Books.

Raven, M. T. (2002). *Mercedes and the chocolate pilot: A true story of the Berlin airlift and the candy that dropped from the sky.* Ann Arbor, MI: Sleeping Bear Press.

ReadWorks. (2000). Should you be afraid of sharks? Retrieved from https://www.readworks.org/article/Should-You-Be-Afraid-of-Sharks/09e4fe4d-b134-425e-8414-e4dd912dba54#!articleTab:content/

ReadWorks. (2007). Battle over the pledge. Retrieved from https://www.readworks.org/article/Battle-Over-the-Pledge/8b625a66-80f8-40e9-8592-2a2c30683520#!articleTab:content/

ReadWorks. (2007). Big dreams. Retrieved from https://www.readworks.org/article/Big-Dreams/58a967c2-be4d-4158-a46c-479582efd5e7#!articleTab:content/

ReadWorks. (2009). A chance for freedom. Retrieved from https://www.readworks.org/article/A-Chance-for-Freedom/98c9875c-6cbb-4db3-86ea-56ddcb15d8bf#!articleTab:content/

ReadWorks. (2009). Taking down the green-eyed monster. Retrieved from https://www.readworks.org/article/Taking-Down-the-Green-Eyed-Monster/c48d52cc-892c-4ab0-8114-d4a7e97704a3#!articleTab:content/

ReadWorks. (2009). World Wonders. Retrieved from https://www.readworks.org/article/World-Wonders/0ea0de31-f95d-4a11-9616-26306bcec498#!articleTab:content/ Wiles, D. (2005). *Freedom summer.* Flushing, NY: Aladdin Books.

ReadWorks. (2014). Letter from Jackie Robinson on civil rights. *ReadWorks.* Retrieved from https://www.readworks.org/article/Letter-from-Jackie-Robinson-on-Civil-Rights/258974c6-0c65-4e71-a457-287259a7ffc9#!articleTab:content/

ReadWorks. (2014). Meet Rosa Parks. *ReadWorks.* Retrieved from https://www.readworks.org/article/Meet-Rosa-Parks/f79794b9-dd04-4adf-8dcb-5aa3b79ca270#!articleTab:content/

ReadWorks. (2014). A tale of segregation: Fetching water. *ReadWorks.* Retrieved from https://www.readworks.org/article/A-Tale-of-Segregation-Fetching-Water/cfdeb9e2-866e-42e9-b476-38b415db0a2d#!articleTab:content/

Reeves, J. (1973). The wind [poem]. In J. Reeves, *Complete Poems for Children.* London: Faber & Faber.

Ross, T. (1997). *Eggbert: The slightly cracked egg.* London: Puffin Books.

Ryder, J. (2015). *Panda kindergarten.* New York: HarperCollins.

Rylant, C. (1988). Spaghetti. In C. Rylant, *Every living thing.* Logan, IA: Perfection Learning.

Sayre, A. P. (2010). *Turtle, turtle, watch out!* Watertown, MA: Charlesbridge.

Schertle, A. (2000). *Down the road.* Boston: HMH Books for Young People.

Steptoe, J. (1987). *Mufaro's beautiful daughters.* New York: Lothrop, Lee & Shepard Books.

Van Allsburg, C. (1986). *The stranger.* Boston: HMH Books for Young People.

Van Allsburg, C. (1991). *The wretched stone.* Boston: Houghton Mifflin.

Wild, M. (2006). *Fox.* San Diego: Kane Miller Book Publishers.

Wiles, D. (2001). *Freedom summer.* New York: Atheneum.

Williams, L. (2017). *The can man.* New York: Lee and Low Books.

Wyeth, S. D. (2002). *Something beautiful.* Decorah, IA: Dragonfly Books.

Yolen, J. (1996). *Encounter.* Boston: HMH Books for Young Readers.

References

ACT Aspire. (n.d.). *Video 1: Exemplar reading items* [Video]. Iowa City: Author. Retrieved from https://www.discoveractaspire.org/assessments/test-items/

Archer, A. L., & Hughes, C. A. (2011). *Explicit instruction: Effective and efficient teaching*. New York: Guilford Press.

Boyles, N. (2004). *Constructing meaning through kid-friendly comprehension strategy instruction*. Gainesville, FL: Maupin House.

Boyles, N. (2012). *That's a GREAT answer: Teaching literature response strategies to elementary, ELL, and struggling readers* (2nd ed.). Gainesville, FL: Maupin House.

Bryner, J. (2012, September 15). What's the difference between alligators and crocodiles? *Live Science*. Retrieved from: https://www.livescience.com/32144-whats-the-difference-between -alligators-and-crocodiles.html

Budiu, R. (2014, July 6). Memory recognition and recall in user interfaces. Nielsen Norman Group. Retrieved from https://www.nngroup.com/articles/recognition-and-recall/

Coleman, D., & Pimentel, S. (2012). Revised publishers' criteria for the Common Core State Standards in English language arts and literacy, grades 3–12. Common Core State Standards Initiative. Retrieved from http://www.corestandards.org/assets/Publishers_Criteria_for _3-12.pdf

Culham, R. (2003). *6+1 traits of writing: The complete guide, grades 3 and up*. New York: Scholastic.

Curriculum Task Force 2.0. (n.d.). Selected response (SR) assessments. Retrieved from http:// ctf2point0.weebly.com/selected-response.html

Glossary of Education Reform. (2014). Formative assessment. Retrieved from http://edglossary .org/formative-assessment/

Henkel, S. A. (2002). Torrance framework for creative thinking [online document]. Available: http://people.bethel.edu/~shenkel/PhysicalActivities/CreativeMovement /CreativeThinking/Torrance.html

Massachusetts Department of Elementary and Secondary Education. English language arts practice tests. *MCAS Resource Center*. Retrieved from http://mcas.pearsonsupport.com /tutorial/practice-tests-ela/

McGraw-Hill. (2015a). *Countdown to Common Core assessments grade 4: English language arts*. New York: Author.

McGraw-Hill. (2015b). *Countdown to Common Core assessments grade 5: English language arts*. New York: Author.

McGraw-Hill. (2015c). *Countdown to Common Core assessments grade 6: English language arts*. New York: Author.

MetaMetrics. (n.d.). *Lexile analyzer*. Retrieved from https://lexile.com/analyzer/

Myhill, D., & Jones, S. (2009). How talk becomes text: Investigating the concept of oral rehearsal in early years' classrooms. *British Journal of Educational Studies, 57*(3), 265–284. Retrieved from https://ore.exeter.ac.uk/repository/bitstream/handle/10036/4474 /2009HowTalkBecomesTextBJES.pdf?sequence=6

Papert, S. (1999). The eight big ideas behind the constructionist learning lab. In G. Stager, *An investigation of constructionism in the Maine youth center* (doctoral dissertation), 2007. Melbourne: University of Melbourne. Retrieved from http://dailypapert.com/may-25-2011-2/

PARCC. (n.d.). ELA test specifications documents. Retrieved from http://parcc-assessment.org /assessments/test-design/ela-literacy/test-specifications-documents

Pearson, P. D. & Gallagher, M. C. (1983). The instruction of reading comprehension. *Contemporary Educational Psychology, 8(3)*, 317–344.

Peterson, P. E., Barrows, S., & Gift, T. (2016). After Common Core, states set rigorous standards. *Education Next*, 16(3). Retrieved from http://educationnext.org/after-common-core-states -set-rigorous-standards/

Robb, L. (2014). *Vocabulary is comprehension: Getting to the root of text complexity.* Thousand Oaks, CA: Corwin.

Sewell, A. (1877). *Black beauty.* Norwich, UK: Jarrold & Sons.

Shanahan, T. (2016, September 2). A fine mess: Confusing close reading and text complexity [blog post]. Retrieved from Center for Development and Learning at http://www.cdl.org /articles/a-fine-mess-confusing-close-reading-and-text-complexity/

Strong, R. W., Silver, H. F., & Perini, M. J. (2001). *Teaching what matters most: Standards and strategies for raising student achievement.* Alexandria, VA: ASCD.

Sztabnik, B. (2015, May 7). A new definition of rigor. *Edutopia.* Retrieved from http://www .edutopia.org/blog/a-new-definition-of-rigor-brian-sztabnik

Texas Education Agency. (n.d.). STAAR released test questions. Retrieved from http://tea.texas .gov/Student_Testing_and_Accountability/Testing/State_of_Texas_Assessments_of _Academic_Readiness_(STAAR)/STAAR_Released_Test_Questions/

Webb, N. (2002, March 28). Depth-of-Knowledge levels for four content areas. Unpublished paper retrieved from Webb's Depth of Knowledge Guide: http://www.aps.edu/re/documents /resources/Webbs_DOK_Guide.pdf

Webb, N. L. (2007). Issues related to judging the alignment of curriculum standards and assessments. *Applied Measurement in Education*, 20(1), 7–25.

Yuan, K., & Le, V. (2012). *Estimating the number of students who were tested on cognitively demanding items through the state achievement tests.* RAND working papers. Arlington, VA: RAND. Retrieved from https://www.rand.org/content/dam/rand/pubs /working_papers/2012/RAND_WR967.pdf

Index

About the Author

 Nancy Boyles is a former classroom teacher and professor emerita at Southern Connecticut State University, where she was professor of reading and graduate reading program coordinator. She now consults with districts and other organizations and agencies, providing workshops, modeling best practices in classrooms, and assisting with curriculum development. Nancy's workshop topics include Close Reading, Small Group Differentiated Instruction, Rigorous Assessment, and Depth of Knowledge.

Nancy is the author of *Closer Reading, Grades 3–6*; *Lessons and Units for Closer Reading, Grades 3–6*; and *Lessons and Units for Closer Reading, K–2*. Nancy has also written many articles and six additional books on reading comprehension.

Nancy's newest program is for small-group close reading instruction in grades 3–5, *Close Reading Links*, published by Capstone. You may contact her at nancyboyles@comcast.net.

Related ASCD Resources: Literacy

At the time of publication, the following resources were available (ASCD stock numbers in parentheses).

Print Products

Achieving Next Generation Literacy: Using the Tests (You Think) You Hate to Help the Students You Love by Maureen Connolly and Vicky Giouroukakis (#116023)

Building Student Literacy Through Sustained Silent Reading by Steve Gardiner (#105027)

A Close Look at Close Reading: Teaching Students to Analyze Complex Texts, Grades K–5 by Diane Lapp, Barbara Moss, Maria Grant, and Kelly Johnson (#114008)

Effective Literacy Coaching: Building Expertise and a Culture of Literacy by Shari Frost, Roberta Buhle, and Camille Blachowicz (#109044)

Engaging Minds in English Language Arts Classrooms: The Surprising Power of Joy by Mary Jo Fresch, Michael F. Opitz, and Michael P. Ford (#113021)

Literacy Leadership for Grades 5–12 by Rosemarye Taylor and Valerie Doyle Collins (#103022)

Literacy Strategies for Grades 4–12: Reinforcing the Threads of Reading by Karen Tankersley (#104428)

Literacy Unleashed: Fostering Excellent Reading Instruction Through Classroom Visits by Bonnie D. Houck and Sandi Novak (#116042)

Read, Write, Lead: Breakthrough Strategies for Schoolwide Literacy Success by Regie Routman (#113016)

Research-Based Methods of Reading Instruction, Grades K–3 by Sharon Vaughn and Sylvia Linan-Thompson (#104134)

Tools for Teaching Writing: Strategies and Interventions for Diverse Learners in Grades 3–8 by David Campos and Kathleen Fad (#114051)

Total Literacy Techniques: Tools to Help Students Analyze Literature and Informational Texts by Pérsida Himmele, William Himmele, and Keely Potter (#114009)

Vocab Rehab: How do I teach vocabulary effectively with limited time? (ASCD Arias) by Marilee Sprenger (#SF114047)

For up-to-date information about ASCD resources, go to **www.ascd.org**. You can search the complete archives of *Educational Leadership* at **www.ascd.org/el**.

ASCD myTeachSource®

Download resources from a professional learning platform with hundreds of research-based best practices and tools for your classroom at http://myteachsource.ascd.org/

For more information, send an e-mail to member@ascd.org; call 1-800-933-2723 or 703-578-9600; send a fax to 703-575-5400; or write to Information Services, ASCD, 1703 N. Beauregard St., Alexandria, VA 22311-1714 USA.